THE ILLUSTRATED LONDON NEWS

SOCIAL HISTORY OF THE FIRST WORLD WAR

Other titles in the same series:

The Illustrated London News
Social History of Victorian Britain
by Christopher Hibbert

The Illustrated London News
Social History of Edwardian Britain
by James Bishop

SOCIAL HISTORY
OF THE FIRST
WORLD WAR

BY JAMES BISHOP

ANGUS & ROBERTSON PUBLISHERS

ANGUS & ROBERTSON PUBLISHERS
London . Sydney . Melbourne . Singapore . Manila

First published in the United Kingdom by Angus &
Robertson (UK) Ltd in 1982

First published in Australia by Angus & Robertson
Publishers in 1982

Foreword Copyright © Lord Blake   1982
Text Copyright © James Bishop   1982
Illustrations © *The Illustrated London News*   1982

ISBN 0 207 14826 0

Picture research and index by Liz Moore
Typeset in 11pt English Times by Setrite Typesetters
Printed in Hong Kong

CONTENTS

ACKNOWLEDGEMENTS

As in the previous volumes in this series most of the illustrations have been reproduced from contemporary issues of *The Illustrated London News*. The others come from *The Sketch, The Graphic, The Sphere* and *The Illustrated Sporting and Dramatic News*, magazines which have ceased publication and which now form part of the archives and picture library of *The Illustrated London News*.

Quotations in the text have been taken from a number of published works, and the author acknowledges his debt to many of the books listed in the Bibliography as well as to the writers of *The Illustrated London News* of the time, many of whom remain anonymous. The quotations from King George V's diary are republished, by gracious permission of Her Majesty the Queen, from Harold Nicolson's biography *King George V*, published by Constable in 1952.

The author also wishes to express his appreciation to Virginia Darbyshire, for her help in researching the book, to Liz Moore, who researched the pictures and compiled the index, and to Liz Falla, who typed the manuscript.

FOREWORD
BY LORD BLAKE

Like Talleyrand; who maintained that the true *douceur de vivre* had been experienced only by those who lived before 1789, mankind has all down history looked back nostalgically to the golden ages of the past. Under the scrutiny of the historian these tend to dissolve into mere dreams, but there is one which deserves some claim to reality: the forty-three years of peace, progress and prosperity between 1871 and 1914 were, for most of Europe anyway, a genuine golden age. It has been compared by one of our most eminent historians to the age of the Antonines. In it there grew up a generation to which war, fanaticism, massacre and revolution, instead of appearing — as they had to nearly every previous generation — typical manifestations of the human spirit, seemed on the contrary to be monstrous deviations from normality. Therefore, when war broke out in 1914 — that terrible war which, despite all the horrors occurring since, still deserves the name of Great — it came as a fiercer shock to civilised Europe than any war before or since. Moreover, it marked the end of an epoch. The year 1914, not 1939, is the true turning point of twentieth-century history, the moment which unleashed the forces of barbarism that are with us still.

How could it have happened? The question has been asked ever since, and answered in a hundred different ways. Was it the fault of Prussian militarism, Russian mobilisation, or French desire for *revanche*? Was Vienna the real culprit, or did a Serbian plot start the whole thing off? Another set of explanations were personal: the Kaiser's jealousy of his uncle's big fleet, the weakness of Bethmann, the recklessness of Conrad, the folly of Sazonov. Then people adduced a whole series of profounder and more cosmic causes: imperialism, capitalism, the old diplomacy, the balance of power, the secret treaties . . . the list is endless. No subject in modern times has had more attention from the historians, and still no simple answer emerges.

Juridically Britain came in because of treaty obligations to Belgium whose neutrality was violated by Germany at the outset of hostilities. No doubt there were deeper reasons of world politics behind the decision, but it was Belgium that swayed a wavering Liberal Cabinet, and Belgium that inspired the enthusiastic indignation of the masses. Belgian atrocities — for the most part the mythical product of propaganda and credulity — formed the staple fare to feed the public wrath. The war was unexpected and took the nation by surprise, but the shock was modified by the confident belief that it would be over with an Allied victory by Christmas and that civilian life would be little affected. This was the great illusion. Kitchener who almost alone prophesied three years underestimated by nearly one third. And as for civilian life, it was never to be the same again.

For this was the first 'total war' in history. The slogan with which it began — 'business as usual' — soon had a hollow ring. Total war means the mobilisation of all the resources of the nation. Even in such an anti-*étatiste* country as the Britain of 1914, the Government half consciously but nevertheless inexorably found itself assuming ever greater powers until by the end it controlled nearly every aspect of civilian as well as military life. This process of taxation, censorship, conscription, and rationing is vividly chronicled in the contemporary pages of *The Illustrated London News* which provide a running commentary on the social changes of the day, all the more effective for being spontaneous and unselfconscious. There is much that seems in retrospect absurd. There was the spymania and the anti-German crusade which was carried to the point of persecuting anyone with a German name, including Prince Louis of Battenberg. The King felt obliged to change the family name to Windsor whereupon the Kaiser, who was not devoid of a sense of humour, is supposed to have said that he would riposte by insisting on Shakespeare's play being re-christened in Germany 'The Merry Wives of Saxe Coburg-Gotha'. Then there was the story that a million Russians were marching through England on their way to the western front in September 1914 and had been seen 'with snow on their boots'.

One notable change brought by total war was the employment of women not only in nursing and similar activities but as auxiliaries to the armed forces and as factory workers. By 1918 there were over 900,000 'munitionettes', as they were nicknamed. War brought emancipation of a sort to many women of all classes hitherto chained by custom to the home. There can be little doubt that sexual promiscuity rose, and was accompanied by an increase in illegitimate births of some thirty per cent. Nor was this the only form of conventionally censured pleasure which became prevalent — 'Eat, drink and be merry for tomorrow we die' became a part of those tortured times along with the huge casualties and the seemingly meaningless slaughter on the western front. When the war ended there was a general sense of moral and physical exhaustion. Two conflicting sentiments shaped the aftermath. There was the hope of a land fit for heroes to live in, but there was also the nostalgia for that Edwardian 'age of the Antonines'. Neither was realised. The legacy of the war was a permanent accretion in the powers of the state, which never returned to their pre-1914 level. The same was to be true of 1939-45. Whether in either case it was 'a good thing' is not for the historian to determine.

Lord Blake

In the month before war broke out this 'Midnight Ball', described at the time as the most successful fancy-dress dance of the season, was held at the Savoy in London. 1

1 THE TERRIBLE CATASTROPHE

The summer of 1914 was uncommonly hot. As August approached most Britons were preoccupied with their arrangements for the coming holiday. The London season was over and the fashionable people who took part in it were leaving town for their country estates or the smart foreign watering places. Others were setting off for Brighton, Blackpool and the other popular seaside resorts. The war clouds gathering over Europe, a phrase which had already stereotyped its way into most newspapers and magazines, were not expected to blow in Britain's direction, though war had been recognised as a possibility — even an inevitability — from the earliest years of the century. The reforms in the Army and Navy which King Edward VII had so strongly supported from the time of his accession were primarily inspired by fear of aggression from abroad, particularly from Germany, though the King had been much concerned in his short reign to try to reassure his nephew, the Kaiser, that the British Government's policy of establishing *ententes cordiales* with France and Russia did not imply any aggressive intent towards Germany.

Neither the British people nor their Government expected to be involved in a war, and when the Cabinet met in July 1914 for a rare discussion on foreign affairs it concluded that, though war seemed likely between the four Continental powers following the Sarajevo assassination, Britain need not be dragged in. The nation was more concerned about the prospect of civil war in Ireland, the effects at home of the 'triple alliance' of miners, transport workers and railwaymen (which had been formed in 1913 and which had threatened to bring the country to a standstill by calling a general strike in support

Most of Britain was on holiday when war was declared in August 1914. This photograph illustrates a new style of bathing dress available that season.   2

August 1914 was exceptionally hot, and this advertisement for the pianola suggested cooler pursuits than tennis and croquet.   3

The Illustrated London News **carried reports and photographs from Sarajevo. This one shows the Archduke Ferdinand and his wife leaving the town hall shortly before he was shot.   4**

2

3

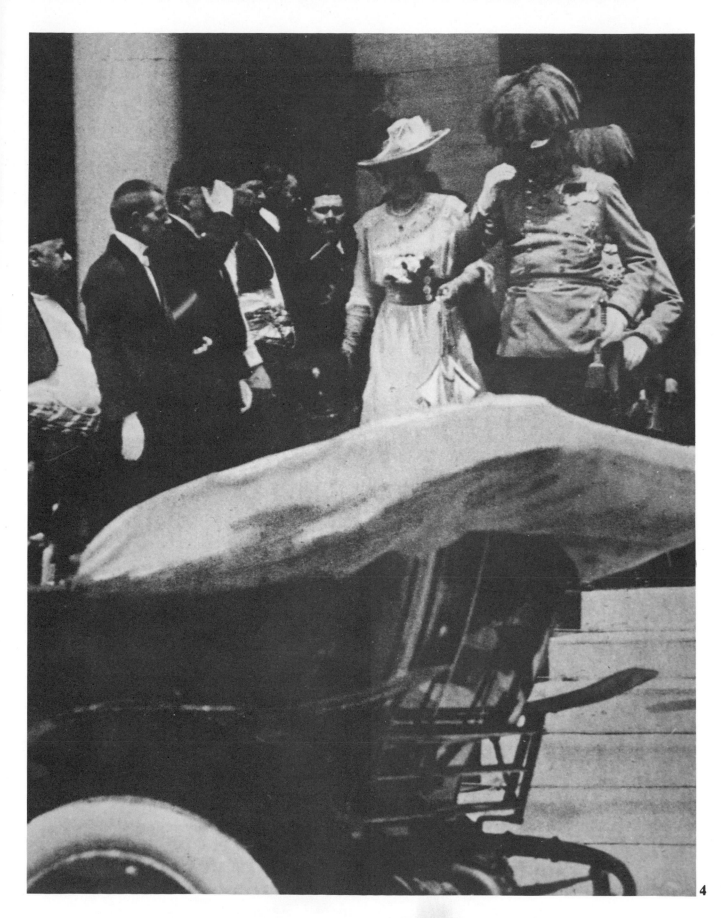

The arrest of one of those involved in the assassination of Archduke Ferdinand.   5

The prospect of civil war in Ireland seemed very close in the summer of 1914 when men of the King's Own Scottish Borderers, who had been rounding up gun-runners, fired on an angry crowd in Dublin. Three people were killed and many more hurt.   6, 7

of their demands for a minimum wage) and the increasing violence of the campaign for women's suffrage. *The Illustrated London News* in July carried scenes from Sarajevo and well-illustrated reports of King George V's inspection of the Fleet at Spithead, but nowhere was there any hint of the catastrophe to come. The paper's parliamentary reports were almost entirely devoted to the Irish question; G.K. Chesterton's columns were pre-occupied with philosophical aspects of the class problem in Britain and divorce in France; there was the first photograph of a diver at the bottom of the sea and some advice on how not to get struck by summer lightning, while the 'Ladies' Page' commented on the fashions displayed at Henley and other traditional events. Not until the issue dated 1 August was it clearly recognised that the 'European war cloud' was ominously close to Britain.

The Illustrated London News was accurately reflecting the mood and opinion of the times. The published memoirs and unpublished recollections of those who were adult enough to be aware of what was going on in 1914 are virtually unanimous in recalling that surprise was their dominant emotion when they learnt that Britain was to be involved in the war. This reaction was shared even by those who might have been expected to have known better, such as the members of the Cabinet. David Lloyd George (who was then Chancellor of the Exchequer) vividly recalled in his war memoirs the ebb and flow of official opinion in Britain:

'When I first heard the news of the assassination of the Grand Duke Ferdinand, I felt that it was a grave matter, and that it might provoke serious consequences which only the firmest and most skilful handling could prevent from developing into an emergency that would involve nations. But my fears were soon assuaged by the complete calm with which the Rulers and diplomats of the world seemed to regard the event. The Kaiser departed for his usual yachting holiday in the Norwegian fiords. His chief Minister left for his usual shooting party on his

King George V on board HMS *Iron Duke* for the inspection of the Fleet at Spithead in July 1914. **8**

8

The first photograph of a diver at the bottom of the sea, published in *The Illustrated London News* of 25 July 1914.   9

Preoccupations of the British at home in the weeks before war broke out: a page of advice on how not to get struck by lightning if caught in a summer storm, and a study of the fashions on display at a polo match at Ranelagh in London.   10, 11

estate in Silesia. The acting Head of the German Foreign Office went off on a honeymoon trip. A still more reassuring fact — the military head of the German Army, von Moltke, left for his cure in a foreign spa. The President of the French Republic and his Prime Minister were on a ceremonial visit to Russia and only arrived back on July 29th. Our Foreign Office preserved its ordinary tranquillity of demeanour and thought it unnecessary to sound an alarm even in the Cabinet Chamber.'

Winston Churchill, who was First Lord of the Admiralty, remembered that it was at a Cabinet meeting on 24 July, called to discuss the Irish crisis, that Ministers were first made aware of the significance of events in Europe. The Cabinet was about to break up when Sir Edward Grey, the Foreign Secretary, read out a document he had just received from the Foreign Office outlining the terms of the Austrian ultimatum to Serbia. Churchill recalled that Grey had been speaking for some time before he could disengage his mind from the 'tedious and bewildering' debate on Ireland. 'We were all very tired,' he wrote in his account in *The World Crisis*, 'but gradually as the phrases and sentences followed one another, impressions of a very different character began to form in my mind.... The parishes of Fermanagh and Tyrone faded back into the mists and squalls of Ireland, and a strange light began to fall and grow upon the map of Europe.'

On 26 July, when Austria rejected Serbia's conciliatory reply to its ultimatum (which Churchill, in a letter to his wife, had described as 'the most insolent document of its kind ever devised'), the dispersal of the British fleets, following their test mobilisation, was halted by the First Sea Lord, Prince Louis of Battenberg. This action was quickly approved by Churchill who returned to London from Cromer where he was holidaying. But though preparations for war now began in earnest, the hope that peace might yet be preserved was kept alive by both politicians and people. Sir Edward Grey's handling of the crisis in the last days of July and the first three of August undoubtedly reflected the mood of the country. There were many demonstrations in favour of peace, culminating in a great public rally in Trafalgar Square on Sunday, 2 August. Lloyd George had reported to the Cabinet that the city, cotton men, industrialists and businessmen were all 'aghast at the bare idea of our plunging into the European conflict'. Nonetheless events seemed to be moving inexorably towards the war that no one wanted. On 31 July the Bank Rate rose from four to eight per cent and the London

12

Mr Winston Churchill was First Lord of the Admiralty when war broke out.   12

Stock Exchange was closed. German yachts were withdrawn from Cowes and later the regatta was abandoned. That Saturday, 1 August, was the beginning of the Bank Holiday weekend and there was a rush to buy food. Prices went up overnight as those with money and storage space went out in cars and taxis to stock up with provisions. Some shops sold out, others imposed their own form of rationing. Ready cash became short and queues

When Austria rejected Serbia's reply to its ultimatum on 26 July Churchill agreed with the First Sea Lord,

Prince Louis of Battenberg, that the Fleet should not be dispersed from the test mobilisation. 13

formed outside the Bank of England as people tried to buy gold.

For many people, already on holiday and away from home, the news was uncertain and aggravatingly slow in coming through. In country districts groups of people would gather outside the local Post Office where short notices might be put up from time to time. Mrs C.S. Peel, in her reminiscences of the domestic life of the period (*How We Lived Then*) recalled that groups of people would sit around on the beach discussing eagerly what news there was. Newspapers were in great demand, and in one village miles from anywhere 'old George, the leader of local opinion, sits in his wheel-back chair on the green and by the light of bicycle lamps reads out the latest tidings'. The Peel family were thankful that they had not gone abroad this year for those that had were beginning to make their way home again as fast as they could. Leonard Woolf recalled in his autobiography (*Beginning Again*) that he first learnt that war was inevitable when bathing at Seaford on Saturday, 1 August. Diving from a raft he came up against a large man with a red face who was swimming out from the beach: 'I apologised and he said to me, almost casually: "Do you know it's war?" We swam side by side for a bit and he told me that he was a London policeman on two weeks holiday, and, although he had had only a few days of his holiday, he had that morning had a telegram recalling him on duty to London. "It's war," he said dejectedly, as we swam towards the beach; "otherwise they wouldn't have recalled me."'

The Cabinet met in emergency session during the Bank Holiday. The Prime Minister, Lord Asquith, recorded in his notes, dated 2 August, that things were pretty black though he was clear in his mind as to what was right and wrong:

'1. We have no obligation of any kind either to France or Russia to give them military or naval help.

2. The dispatch of the Expeditionary Force to help France at this moment is out of the question and would serve no object.

3. We must not forget the ties created by our long-standing and intimate friendship with France.

4. It is against British interests that France should be wiped out as a Great Power.

5. We cannot allow Germany to use the Channel as a hostile base.

6. We have obligations to Belgium to prevent it being utilized and absorbed by Germany.'

On 3 August Sir Edward Grey addressed a crowded House of Commons to explain the situation. The scene was described by Michael MacDonagh, a member of the parliamentary reporting staff of *The Times*, who noted that a sense of national emergency was now keenly realised, and observed, from the window of his tram bringing him to the House from his home in Clapham, an *Evening Standard* bill carrying the line 'On the Brink of Catastrophe'. But he also noted that his fellow passengers seemed more excited than alarmed:

'The Chamber was indeed packed today, floor and galleries, by Members and public,' he recorded in his diary (*In London during the Great War*). 'It was pervaded by that subtle emotional element so noticeable in the House on great occasions when feeling, despite the desire to keep it under control, is too strong to be wholly subdued. There was a deep hum of conversation, and Members moved uneasily in their places. Gravity with an undertone of anxiety was the prevailing mood. The chief personage of the occasion was already in his place — Sir Edward

As war became imminent German yachts were withdrawn from Cowes and the traditional regatta was abandoned.   14

Grey, sitting on the Treasury Bench with Asquith, Prime Minister, on his right hand and Lloyd George, Chancellor of the Exchequer, to his left. So finely chiselled and pale is Grey's handsome face that it is like carved ivory. His demeanour, like his face, is calm and cold. His air of distinction prepossesses one in his favour. He looks what he is — the perfect gentleman.

'Grey on rising got a prolonged cheer from both sides of the House, and he stood at the Table — tall and erect in his light summer suit — until the applause had subsided and the House settled down to listen. It was a plain statement of the events that had led to the crisis, to which the tremendous issue — Peace or War? — imparted a solemn seriousness. Nor was he long in coming to the point. Great Britain was pledged to maintain the integrity of Belgium under the treaty signed by the Powers in 1839. So were France and Germany. We were bound in honour therefore to stand by our plighted word. Moreover, we had a vital interest in the maintenance of the independence of Belgium as a friendly buffer

state nearest to our shores. If there was to be a War, he said, Great Britain would suffer terribly. But if we were to stand aside it would mean the loss of our self-respect, and at the end of the War we should find ourselves powerless to prevent Europe falling under the domination of one Power, to our undoing.

'Enough! The central figure of the scene was no longer the dignified presence of Sir Edward Grey, but a portent which presented itself to the mind's eye — the horrid spectre of War!'

The public mood changed rapidly when it became

'The war clouds hanging over Europe' discussed in the Foreign Office. Standing, left, Sir Edward Grey, the British Foreign Secretary, with Count Benckendorff, the Russian Ambassador. Seated, left, M. Paul Cambon, the French Ambassador, with Prince Lichnowsky, the German Ambassador and, right, Count Mensdorff-Pouilly-Dietrichstein, the Austro-Hungarian Ambassador (left) with the Marquis Imperiali di Francarcha, Italian Ambassador. 15

16

Belgian refugees prepare to leave Antwerp en route to England after the Germans besieged their city.   16, 17

17

known that Germany was violating the neutrality of Belgium and that the British Government had sent an ultimatum to Germany demanding the withdrawal of its troops by midnight of 4 August. Once more large crowds assembled in London, but this time instead of demonstrating for peace they shouted their support for Belgium and for the British Government's stand. A hostile crowd gathered outside the German Embassy and smashed the windows and police had some difficulty in restoring order. Elsewhere the crowds were generally good-humoured, and as the hour for the expiry of the ultimatum (11 p.m. in Britain) drew near they gathered outside Downing Street and Buckingham Palace, where the King held a meeting of the Privy Council at 10.45 p.m. He later wrote in his diary:

Crowds outside Buckingham Palace cheer the King and Queen on the night of the declaration of war. 'A mighty cheer' went up when the King and Queen appeared on the balcony, *The Illustrated London News* **reported, and the crowd 'sang the National Anthem with the utmost fervour'. 18**

Crowds press round the car carrying the Prime Minister, Mr Asquith, to Downing Street. 19

18

19

20

21

22

The 2nd Battalion of the Grenadier Guards in battle kit march past Buckingham Palace on their way to France.   20

Prince Lichnowsky, the German Ambassador, shortly before his departure from London following the outbreak of war.   21

The brass plate is removed from the German Embassy at 9, Carlton House Terrace, London.   22

'Tuesday August 4. I held a Council at 10.45 to declare war with Germany. It is a terrible catastrophe, but it is not our fault. An enormous crowd collected outside the Palace; we went on the balcony both before and after dinner.'

The Daily News described the scene more graphically:

'The enthusiasm culminated outside Buckingham Palace when it became known that war had been declared. The word was passed round by the police that silence was necessary, inasmuch as the King was holding a Council for the signing of the necessary proclamations .... The news that war had been declared was received with tremendous cheering which grew into a deafening roar when King George, Queen Mary and the Prince of Wales appeared on the balcony.

'Westminster, Charing Cross and the main thoroughfares round Westminster were thronged all last night with excited throngs, who displayed marked tendencies towards mafficking . . . Union Jacks were everywhere to be seen, and the air was filled with the sound of patriotic songs.'

The crowds that gathered so enthusiastically outside Buckingham Palace were less aware than their King of the terrible catastrophe that was beginning to unfold. Few appreciated that war would be no longer a matter simply for the professional services; that there would be, in a phrase soon to be coined, a 'home front' for civilians as well as a front on which the armies fought; and that the social and domestic life of the

Austrian reservists answering the call to arms at the Austro-Hungarian consulate in London. 23

nation would be transformed with ordinary people subjected to regulation, discomfort and privation such as had not been experienced before. But on the night of 4 August it was assumed that the war would not last more than a few months, that it would be fought in conventional fashion between regular armies and navies, and that the lives of the ordinary citizen would be little affected. On such widely believed, but totally false, assumptions Britain went to war — a war which, as Lloyd George noted at the time, seemed to be universally acclaimed and which was declared when the nation was officially on holiday.

Mr Asquith (standing in the doorway) saw M. Millerand, the French Minister of War (entering the car) and the French Commander-in-Chief, General Joffre, during a visit to British headquarters in France.   24

The Kaiser, as Supreme Commander of the German Army, photographed inspecting his troops at the front with the German Chief of Staff, General von Moltke.   25

24

2 YOUR COUNTRY NEEDS YOU

The coming of war brought a great deal of hubbub and excitement, but analysis of the frenzied activity during the first few months of war at home shows that much of it was not very constructive. Everybody wanted to be doing something but the fact was that there was not, immediately, very much to do. The call-up of the reserves changed the habits of many homes but those who were not affected could not at first find any useful contribution to make. Civilians and retired servicemen anxious to take some part in the defence of their country discovered in these early days — as Mrs Peel noted — that

On the declaration of war the Government was empowered compulsorily to purchase and mobilise horses from civilian owners. These horses were taken from the stables of W.H. Smith and Sons, the news agents, in London.   26

Loading ammunition onto a requisitioned bus from the Powder Magazine in Hyde Park.   27

26

27

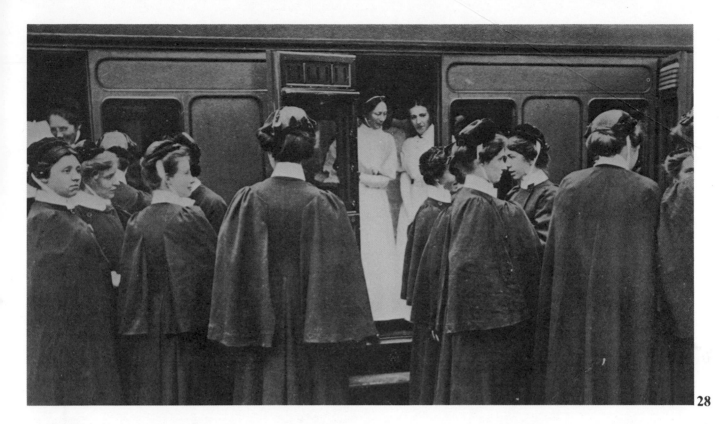

28

A party of London nurses at Charing Cross station preparing to leave for the front.   28

A National Relief Fund was set up by the Prince of Wales, and more than a million pounds had been collected within two weeks. The coupon was carried by most publications at the time, urging people to return it with their contribution to Buckingham Palace. Other appeals were launched to relieve the distress of war among the families of soldiers and sailors and for many other causes.   29

YOU ARE ASKED TO FILL THIS UP.

I enclose £   s.   d. toward the Prince of Wales's

NATIONAL   RELIEF   FUND.

Name..

Address..

....

This coupon should be filled in, and the envelope, which need not be stamped, addressed to H.R.H. The Prince of Wales, Buckingham Palace, London.   29

worried and puzzled officials 'appeared to have no plans regarding the utilization of any services but those of soldiers, sailors and hospital nurses'.

There was a burgeoning of committees and working parties. The Prince of Wales launched the National Relief Fund in anticipation of unemployment and food shortages, and within two weeks it had accumulated more than a million pounds. Several funds were established to provide help for Belgian refugees and there were appeals to help relieve the distress of war among the families of soldiers and sailors, and for many other worthy causes. The Queen appealed to all the needlework guilds in the country to send in underclothing for soldiers and sailors. In one neighbourhood a working party of women was established to make baby clothes for soldiers' and sailors' wives, not because there was suddenly a greater need for baby clothes, but because it gave people the opportunity to get together to talk about the war news, such as it was, and to feel useful.

Arnold Bennett recorded in his *Journal* of the time both his eagerness for news (he had telegrams from a news agency sent to Thorpe-le-Soken from London each day which were displayed in the local

Post Office) and the almost desperate activities of local people: hiding their silver, moving boats inland, organising the local rifle club in case of a German invasion, and a farmer 'laying in ammunition against the time when the populace will raid the country demanding provisions'. He noted, on 6 August, that petrol was fetching up to 10s a tin at Clacton; that there was a slight increase at the fish shop in the prices of poultry and eggs; that farmers in the neighbourhood appeared to have raised the price of butter by threepence a pound; that a firm at Clacton was reported to be making an extra £50 a week by unjustified increases in the price of bread; and that there was a great activity of dispatch-riders on motor-bikes who were, he thought, the most picturesque feature of the war in those parts, rushing through the village at speeds estimated up to

Nurses leaving the War Office after receiving their orders.   30

Selling flags for the French Red Cross.   31

In its courtyard the Bank of England issued prospectuses for the 4½ per cent War Loan.   32

A seventeenth century rifle presented by the King was sold at Christies in 1915 in aid of the Red Cross.   33

A call for gloves and mittens for troops at the front was launched soon after war began by women described as

being 'well known and very popular in English Society'.   **34**

35

36

The Duchess of Westminster at her sewing machine in the grounds of her home in Roehampton, preparing clothing for the field hospital she equipped for the front.   35

Boy Scouts in Birmingham volunteered to help with the building of huts and stables for use by the War Office, and their offer was accepted.   36

fifty miles an hour (Bennett himself was willing to concede forty).

Bennett's friend, H.G. Wells, wrote to *The Times* urging the British public to organise itself against invasion and to be prepared to take to guerilla warfare if need be. Wells was impatient with the official view that fighting was for the armed forces. 'Let the expert have no illusions as to what we ordinary people are going to do if we find German soldiers in England one morning,' he wrote. 'We are going to fight . . . . If the experts attempt any pedantic interference, we will shoot the experts.' *The Times* itself ran a column of 'Practical Patriotism — How to be useful in Wartime', which, among other things, listed defence organisations and the growing number of charities to which gifts could be sent.

Those living on the south and east coasts were most aware of the official alarm in the early days of the war at the possibility of invasion. Barbed wire

Minesweepers at work in the North Sea, and a destroyer in the Channel provides a tow for a British dirigible whose engine broke down while on patrol duty. 37, 38

was threaded along the beaches, piers were destroyed or cut in half to prevent their use for landing troops, some buildings were blown up either because they were too prominent as landmarks, or too tempting targets, or because they blocked the fields of fire of the defending forces. Lights along the seafronts were turned off, and for a short time even lighthouses and lightships were extinguished. Printed instructions were prepared for local inhabitants advising them how to behave if the enemy invaded. At Hove the *Instructions to Inhabitants* cautioned people to stay at home unless they were ordered to move by the military, in which case they should proceed north-west over the Downs, taking to fields where necessary. In such circumstances they were advised to take money, food and blankets with them. Elsewhere citizens were told how to make sure that vehicles and livestock were rendered useless to the invaders and in country districts there were many reports of the Army commandeering vehicles and horses for military use, including farm horses needed for the harvest.

37

38

39

Those living on the south and east coasts of England were the first to be made aware of the dangers of war. This mine was washed up on the east coast during the first weeks of the war, though its exact location was censored.   39

Advertisers were not slow to adjust to wartime conditions and opportunities.   40

40

In the cities the rush for food remained the principal preoccupation. Michael MacDonagh found the food departments of both the Army and Navy and the Civil Service stores in London thronged with buyers on the day after war was declared, all of them armed with what appeared to be abnormally long lists of groceries. He also noted a slight rise in prices, but that was a secondary consideration, for it was generally supposed that the pinch of war would first be felt in scarcity of food. The fact that there was a general increase in food prices during the first days was later recorded by the *Annual Register*, which published this list of comparative prices between 28 July and 6 August:

	July 28	August 6
Flour	1¼d	1½d
Sugar	1¾d	4d
Beef	6½d	7½d
Beef (chilled)	6d	7½d
Beef (frozen)	4½d	6½d
Mutton	8d	8½d
Bacon	8½d	10½d
Cheese	6¾d	8½d
Butter	1s 1d	1s 3d

There was considerable public outcry both about prices and about the hoarding of food. The Government responded by imposing limits on retail prices and by declaring that there was no shortage of food. And, as a general example to the nation, it was announced that by order of the King and Queen plain, simple living was to be the rule at the royal table.

On the official side the preoccupation, in the early months of the war, was with the call to arms. The Liberal Secretary of State for War, Colonel Seely, had resigned shortly before war was declared and on 5 August the Prime Minister persuaded Lord Kitchener, former Commander-in-Chief of the British forces in the Boer War and currently British Representative in Egypt, to take the post. Always a popular hero, Kitchener's appointment did more than anything else to persuade the public of the British Government's determination to wage the war professionally. On the day after his appointment the first recruiting posters were issued. They carried the slogan 'Your King and Country Need You', and were printed in red, white and blue. Underneath the heading were the words: 'In this crisis our Country

MILK & SUGAR BOTH UP!

Follow "Truth's" advice :

"TRUTH" recommends : "Careful house-wives to be chary of sugar and economise in every convenient way. **CONDENSED MILK** . . . . . is useful in this direction, and **lends itself to far more methods of cookery than it is as a rule used for.**"

PROVE THIS YOURSELF :
BUY A TIN OF

NESTLÉ'S MILK

NO ALTERATION IN PRICE

and send a post card for " Dainty Dishes " and other information supplied gratis on application.

NESTLÉ'S, EASTCHEAP, LONDON, E.C.

By
Appointment

to
H.M. the King.

41

calls on her young unmarried men to rally round the Flag and enlist in the ranks of the Army' — the age limit was eighteen to thirty years. Another poster carried the heading 'A Call to Arms' and declared: 'An addition of 100,000 men to His Majesty's Regular Army is immediately necessary in the present grave national emergency.' The famous portrait of Kitchener with the pointing finger was added later. In the term of service, which was for a period of three years or until the war was concluded, Kitchener showed that he did not share the general view that the war would be over by Christmas. The initial call for 100,000 men was answered within a month with queues of volunteers assembling outside recruiting offices all over the country. On 28 August another 100,000 men were called for, the age limit being raised to thirty-five years of age, and a special

Food shortages and complaints of hoarding and rises in prices were an early feature of the war at home, hence the Nestle advertisement's emphasis on 'no alteration in price'. 41

'No household in the land lives more plainly' was the caption given to this illustration of a lunch at Sandringham, following the official announcement, by order of the King and Queen, that simple living was to be the rule at the royal table. 42

42

The Prince of Wales, who joined the 3rd Battalion of the Grenadier Guards immediately after the declaration of war, went to France as ADC to Sir John French.   43

The Officers' Training Corps of Westminster School on parade.   44

44

A parade of new recruits at Liverpool in March 1915 was inspected by Lord Kitchener, the Secretary of War, as part of his recruitment campaign.   45

The Kitchener recruiting poster.   46

"YOUR COUNTRY NEEDS YOU"

appeal was made to married men. Two weeks later Parliament authorised a further increase of half a million men.

The call was answered by the country's young men in a wave of enthusiasm and not a little popular pressure, reflected in such popular songs as 'We don't want to lose you, But think you ought to go', and declarations such as that put out by the London Parliamentary Recruiting Committee: 'There are three types of men. Those who Hear the Call and Obey; Those who Delay; And The Others. To which Do You Belong?' There were few 'others'. Rupert Brooke undoubtedly reflected the mood of the country when he wrote:

Honour has come back, as a king, to earth,
    And paid his subjects with a royal wage;
And Nobleness walks in our ways again;
    And we have come into our heritage.

'We don't want to lose you, but think you ought to go.' Volunteers outside the recruiting office at Camberwell Town Hall.   47

Volunteers from the Empire. A troopship is seen off from Victoria, British Columbia.   48

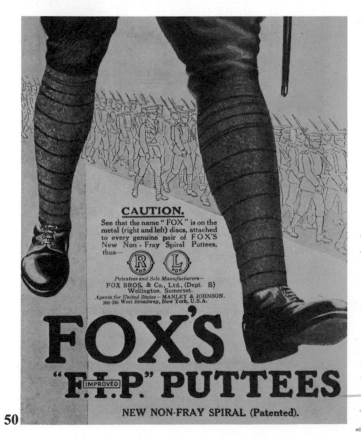

The Carlton Hotel in London lent its support to the recruiting drive.   49

Advertisement for regulation puttees.   50

In support of the Government's War Loan model warships were floated in the fountains of Trafalgar Square.   51

In spite of its success Kitchener's appeal was not enough to meet the demands of the western front. The heavy casualties in 1915 meant that 700,000 volunteers were insufficient to fill the trenches. The Cabinet remained undecided on the issue of conscription and, in an attempt to preserve the voluntary system, introduced the Derby Scheme. Lord Derby, Under-Secretary of State for War, was appointed Director of Recruitment in October 1915 with the task of canvassing the country's manpower. Persuasion rather than compulsion was the principle of the Derby Scheme, by which every man between the age of eighteen and forty-one was called upon to 'attest' — to undertake to enlist when required to do

so. Attested men were divided into the single men and the married, but certain starred occupations (munitions workers, coal miners, industrial workers, merchant seamen, public utility employees) were exempted. The scheme has been described as a gigantic engine of fraud and moral blackmail and it did not succeed in its objective. When it ended, in December 1915, only 343,000 eligible men had attested in spite of a special appeal by the King and the accounts in *The Illustrated London News* reporting long queues of men eager to be attested. In fact most of those who did so turned out to be

Lord Derby, who was appointed Director of Recruiting in October 1915, launched a further campaign for recruitment by persuasion rather than compulsion, calling for men to 'attest' — meaning they would agree to enlist when required to do so. The scheme failed to produce enough recruits and conscription then became inevitable. 52

Queues of men waiting to be attested during the last week of Lord Derby's scheme in December 1915. 53

53

54

The Military Cross was introduced as a new war decoration in 1915. 54

Bovril links itself to the recruiting campaign. 55

British Bull :—

"*My* place is at the front—

"**I hear they**
"**want more**
"**BOVRIL**"

BRITISH TO THE BACKBONE

55

married men and more than a million bachelors failed to make the commitment.

Conscription now seemed to be inevitable to many, though its necessity and desirability were not recognised by all. There was, nonetheless, widespread concern at the lengths to which persuasion was being taken. Recruiting posters were frequently aimed at women. One, headed 'To the young women of London', read:

'Is your "Best Boy" wearing khaki? If not, don't you think he should be?

'If he does not think that you and your country are worth fighting for — do you think he is worthy of you?

'Don't pity the girl who is alone; her young man is probably a soldier, fighting for her and his country — and for YOU.'

Another call to the 'Women of England', read:

'When the War is over and your husband or your son is asked — What did you do in the Great War? — is he to hang his head because *you* would not let him go?

'Women of England, do your duty! Send your men today to join our Glorious Army.'

An 'Active Service League' was founded by Baroness Orczy, the celebrated author of the 'Scarlet Pimpernel' books. It devised a pledge which women were urged to sign: 'At this hour of England's grave peril and desperate need I do hereby pledge myself most solemnly in the name of my King and Country to persuade every man I know to offer his services to the country, and I also pledge myself never to be seen in public with any man who, being in every way fit and free for service, has refused to respond to his country's call.'

Other groups of women formed themselves into the 'Order of the White Feather' which they publicly conferred upon any young man they found wearing civilian clothes.

In such an atmosphere of enthusiasm it was perhaps not surprising that on occasion recruiting officers acted beyond the normal bounds of duty. In the House of Commons, in July 1915, a complaint was made by James Hogge, Liberal Member for

Recruiting poster issued by the Parliamentary Recruiting Committee.   56

The Illustrated London News published this drawing contrasting the satisfaction of the man who had enlisted with the unease of the man who had not, in November 1915, in support of the Derby Scheme.   57

East Edinburgh, about a letter sent by a local recruiting officer to a potential recruit which seemed to suggest not just that his country needed him but was coming to get him. The letter, as read to the House, said:

Dear Sir,
    Unless you have some good and genuine reason for not enlisting, which I am agreeable to investigate, I advise you to offer to join the Army before you are made to. This is an entirely private and friendly piece of advice. Compulsion may not be so far off as you think. I am only waiting the word to call up every man of eligible age and as you can see I have you on my list.
    I can only tell you that I have good reason to

believe that you will be mightily sorry in the end if you wait until you are fetched. Not only that, but if it comes to fetching, those who are fetched will not be asked where they would like to go.

The Minister responsible, Walter Long, assured the House that recruiting officers had no authority for issuing such threats, and said he hoped there would be no more letters of this kind. But the

controversy underlined the Government's dilemma. There had never been conscription in Britain before, and many Liberal MPs in the Coalition believed that any attempt to introduce it would divide the country. They saw it as fundamentally undemocratic. G.K. Chesterton, who had been writing the 'Our Notebook' feature in *The Illustrated London News* since 1905 until his illness in November 1914 resumed the weekly column, on his recovery in mid-1915, with no such doubts. On 12 June he wrote

that, at this moment, a patriot would not wish for anything except to get the better of the Germans. 'Whether conscription will help or hinder us in that is a matter for the authorities; and a very difficult matter even for them. If they want it we must give it them, not because they are the best conceivable people who could decide, but because they are the only people who can decide. If we are always whining for a man with "a genius for governing" we are simply proving ourselves destitute of an equally

noble gift — a genius for being governed.... When we come to the stage of decision we must do as we are told, as every democracy in the world is doing; and the firmer the democracy the firmer the discipline.'

Chesterton returned to the subject in a subsequent column: 'I strongly object to bad arguments even for good causes — or rather, especially for good causes. And in those rare but real cases in which something like a good cause can be made out on both sides, I object to them most of all. One of these is conscription: and now that the practical problem is in the hands of the authorities I think it would be well if we carted away the lumber of bad arguments that have served for barricades on both sides. To show I am not leaning here towards anything but logic, I will take two fallacies flourishing on alternative sides. First, for instance, there is not only no truth, but there is scarcely any meaning, in the statement of some Liberals that conscription is a

denial of democracy. Democracy is the achievement of what the people want; and the people have as much right to want conscription as to want anything else. And seeing that the most democratic country in the world, our own Ally, France, not only has long had conscription, but practically invented conscription, it is irrational to say that the thing is against democracy, though there might be a certain sense in saying it is against liberty. Now the old Liberal answer to the statement that France had conscription was the perfectly fair one that she would not have it if she could help it. But as we are now admittedly in an abnormal crisis and need an abnormal army, this Liberal answer is in its turn quite fairly answered by saying that *we* also would not have it if *we* could help it, but that we can't help it. Admittedly the thing might be necessary; and a necessary conscription cannot in itself destroy English democracy, unless it has already destroyed French democracy.

59

The Government finally decided on compulsory military service in January 1916. The Bill was introduced in the House of Commons on 5 January, and had its third reading on 24 January, when 383 MPs voted in favour and thirty-six against. The drawing shows the scene during the vote in the House. 58
Announcement of the call-up. 59

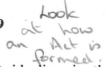

'But if the anti-Militarists put idealism in the wrong place, the Militarists do so also, in an even more sentimental and extravagant degree. I call it rank sentimentalism, for instance, to talk about the ''injustice'' of taking several soldiers from one family and no soldiers from another family. What we want is not ''justice'' — or rather, arithmetic — but soldiers, and especially good soldiers. Now, it is a known fact that good soldiers very often go in families; all of us know that surnames cover six or seven brothers and cousins practically all of whom are trusted and experienced soldiers. I can conceive nothing more unpractical, and certainly nothing more unmilitary, than to miss one of these men in order to drag somebody else out of bed, or from under the bed.'

The Government, though reluctant to do so, had itself recognised that conscription might become inevitable. Soon after the Derby Scheme began

Asquith had pointed to the possible consequences: 'If,' he declared in the House of Commons on 2 November 1915, 'there should still be found a substantial number of men of military age not required for other purposes, and who, without excuse, hold back from the service of their country, I believe that the very same conditions which make compulsion impossible now — namely the absence of general consent — would force the country to a view that they must cease to supplement, by some form of legal obligation, the failure of the voluntary system.' That legal obligation came two months later when, on 5 January 1916, Asquith introduced the Military Service Bill. In spite of the obvious need for more men at the front the Bill roused a good deal of political opposition, including a split within the ranks of the Liberal Government. The Home Secretary, Sir John Simon, resigned and several others, including the Chancellor of the Exchequer and the Foreign Secretary, threatened to do so. Nonetheless the Bill became law before the end of January. It provided for the call-up of single men and childless widowers aged between eighteen and forty. In March the call-up was extended to married men who had attested under the Derby Scheme and, as a result of complaints that some unmarried men were evading service, the National Union of Attested Married Men was formed to campaign for equality of sacrifice.

By April 1916 it had become evident that these measures were not sufficient to provide the required reinforcements and a new crisis in the Government was heralded when Lloyd George, who had been appointed Minister of Munitions in March of the previous year, threatened to resign unless all men of military age were made liable to conscription. Following two secret sessions in the House of Commons, during which the Prime Minister was apparently convinced that such a measure would not be too politically divisive, nor produce the social upheaval in the country that he had feared, a Bill was introduced to impose immediate and general conscription. It passed through the House of

In February 1917 the Government called for volunteer workers for trades of national importance intended to replace those called from national industries for military service. National Service 'forms of offer' were issued from post offices.   60

A tank, supported by an airship dropping leaflets, was the centre of a campaign in Trafalgar Square in support of the War Loan, in March 1918.   61, 62

60

61

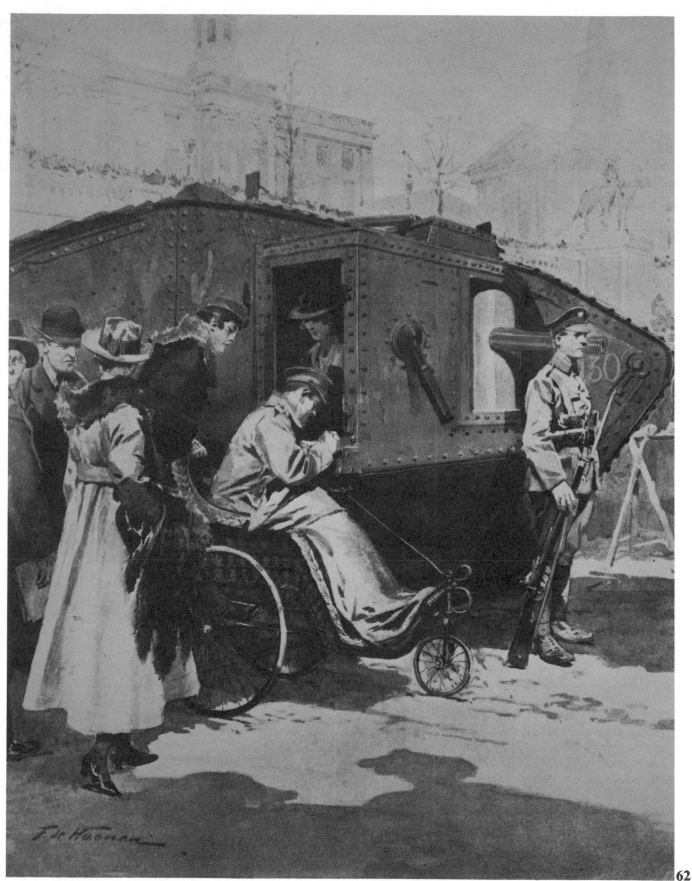

F. de Haenen

Commons with only thirty-seven MPs voting against it, and received the Royal Assent on 25 May. Tribunals were set up to adjudicate on claims for exemption, and 'conscientious objection', a new phrase in the English vocabulary, became a burning issue. Mrs Pankhurst recorded that those who refused to wear khaki, having been turned down by the tribunals, were bullied and terrorised. In July the council of Trinity College, Cambridge, removed Bertrand Russell from his lectureship in logic and mathematics shortly after he had been fined £100 for making statements calculated to prejudice recruiting. Altogether it has been estimated that there were some 16,000 conscientious objectors, of whom perhaps a quarter accepted service in the Non-Combatant Corps, rather fewer did ambulance work and about 1,300 went to prison. Among those who defended the right of the individual to protest against the demands of the state and the majority were F.W. Hirst, editor of *The Economist*, and Dr John Clifford, the Baptist Minister who, before the war, had sought to organise passive resistance against the payment of education rates and who now, though wholeheartedly supporting the fight against Germany, was equally wholehearted in his opposition to conscription. It was, he declared, a fraud. 'It does not express the mature judgment of the people. . . . Conscience is the best asset a nation can possess.'

Chesterton had some trenchant comments to make on the conscientious objector in a column published in *The Illustrated London News* in May 1918. He might more properly be called an unconscientious objector, Chesterton suggested, 'for he does not so much believe in his own conscience as disbelieve in the common conscience which is the soul of any possible society. His hatred of patriotism is very much plainer than his love for peace. But just as the instantaneous touch of ice has been mistaken for hot iron, so the unnatural chilliness of his personality is sometimes mistaken for fanaticism. The most horribly unholy and unhappy thing about him is his youth. Most of the more representative Pacifists are old men — and indeed, saving their presence, old noodles. But they are kindly old noodles. . . . No such lingering grace clings to the young man I have in mind. He is cold, he is caddish, he is an intellectual bully, and his intellect is itself vapid and thin. . . he is a pacifist not because he is a Quaker, or because he is a Tolstoyan, or even because he is an Anarchist — but because he is a prig, and nothing else. Nor is he even a prig through too much conscientiousness, or a pedant through too much learning. He has nothing but

Military hospital in Cambridge. 63

ideas which are not only second-rate, but second-hand.'

Chesterton's views undoubtedly reflected those of the vast majority of his countrymen. The war had to be won, and victory had to be total; there was little tolerance of any opposing view. The demands of the

63

trenches along the western front were inexorable and by 1918 men of up to fifty-one years were being called up, as were many men who had previously been in reserved occupations. Field-Marshal Lord French, Commander-in-Chief on the home front, declared that in making all necessary preparations to repel an invasion he was considering the formation of a compulsory militia for all men up to the age of sixty. Britain had become by this time, as one contemporary observer noted, a country of women, old men and children, with a sprinkling of men in khaki and the light blue uniforms of the wounded.

3 DEFENDING THE REALM

In Britain one of the greatest changes brought about by the war was a dramatic increase of state control over men's lives. Until 1914, as A.J.P. Taylor noted in his *English History 1914-1945*, a 'sensible, law-abiding Englishman could pass through life and hardly notice the existence of the state, beyond the post office and the policeman'. It was certainly true that the Englishman, or any inhabitant of the British Isles, could live where he liked and as he liked, could leave the country without permission and come back into it whenever he wished, could travel abroad without a passport and exchange currency without restriction. But in some ways the precedent of state interference had already been set before 1914. If a man earned more than £160 a year he had to pay income tax (a burden imposed on only a small minority at that time, for the average income of a male industrial worker when war broke out was £75 a year). Education was compulsory up to the age of twelve, and the state provided free school meals and free school medical services. The state also

64

To avert financial panic and discourage people from hoarding gold sovereigns the Treasury, at the beginning of the war, was empowered to issue paper notes. This note was issued in October 1914.   **64**

Postal censorship at work. A tube containing coffee beans was found hidden in a roll of newspapers addressed to Germany, in contravention of a ban on the export of foodstuffs to the enemy.   **65**

Mr F.E. Smith, MP, was the first Director of the Press Bureau but left for active service at the end of September 1914.   **66**

65

67

The Prisoners of War Information Bureau — a Government department set up to keep a record of all British prisoners of war in Germany.   67

provided, under the Old Age Pensions Act of 1908, a pension of 5s a week for the needy over seventy years of age and since 1911 had helped to insure workers against sickness and unemployment. The onset of war greatly intensified state activity. The Government's first acts were designed to avert financial panic. In order to discourage people from hoarding gold sovereigns the Treasury was empowered to issue paper notes in denominations of £1 and 10s. The Government also took over the insurance of war risks on shipping and responsibility for bills on neutral and enemy countries as well as assuming control of the railways.

On 8 August 1914 the Defence of the Realm Act (commonly known as DORA) was passed, putting Britain under martial law. The executive was provided with almost unlimited powers by this Act and its subsequent provisions. Police were empowered to stop and question suspects and to imprison people who refused to stop and answer questions. Offences 'committed with the intention of assisting the enemy' were punishable by death. Newspapers ran the risk of prosecution if they published unauthorised news or speculated about strategy or the conduct of the war, and on 10 August a Press Bureau was set up, under F.E. Smith MP (later Lord Birkenhead). The Press Bureau was for the twin purposes of issuing official war news supplied by the

War Office and the Admiralty and of censoring any war news that the newspapers might obtain for themselves. In the early months of the war this did not amount to much, for Lord Kitchener refused to allow war correspondents at the front. The dispatch of the British Expeditionary Force to France in August was carried out without the knowledge of the majority of the British people, and the news of their retreat at the end of August was ultimately released by the Bureau (with some embellishments put in by Smith himself) with the intention of emphasising the need for reinforcements in France. The Bureau was set up in the Royal United Service Institution in Whitehall. Michael MacDonagh described its operation:

'The Press Room of the Bureau is in the theatre of the Institution, to which entrance is obtained by a door in the back in Whitehall Gardens. Here representatives of the London and country daily papers, and the news agencies, are in attendance day and night, so as to be ready to transmit news as it comes in, without delay, to their head offices, each of which has a telephone box communicating with it directly. Typewritten copies of the news are distributed simultaneously to the Press representatives. Accordingly they all start fair in the rush to their telephone boxes, competition being keen, particularly among the evening paper men, to be in first with the news. The Chief Censor is E.T. Cook, an able and experienced journalist who has been editor in succession of the *Daily News*, *Pall Mall Gazette* and *Westminster Gazette*. I have had to see him frequently at the Bureau about articles written for my paper by various people for which the immediate endorsement "Passed by the Censor" was requested. Two proofs of such articles are sent to the Bureau. One is kept at the Bureau for comparison with the article as published to see if the Censor's alterations, if any, have been made. Cook impresses me as a cool, cautious, critical person — the kind of editor who produces a very accurate paper but perhaps rather a dull one. He is well fitted for seeing that war news is given in its bare bones without distortion, without exaggeration and without colour.'

As invariably happens when censorship is imposed the blue pencil seems to have been exercised in an unnecessarily cautious, and often arbitrary, manner. Some examples of this censorship in action were raised in the House of Commons in questions to the Home Secretary, Sir John Simon, who was responsible to Parliament for the operation of the Press Bureau. One celebrated example was the removal, from a descriptive article sent by a cor-

The Battle of Loos, September 1915. An artist's impression, published in _The Illustrated London News_, shows British troops, wearing gas masks, charging the German lines. John Buchan's account of the engagement, in which he praised the valour shown by some German soldiers, was censored. 68

respondent from the front line when Kitchener's ban had been withdrawn, of the reference to kings in Rudyard Kipling's line 'The Captains and the Kings depart', which was quoted in the dispatch. The blue pencil was put through the words 'and the Kings'. In his reply to a question in the House the Home Secretary said that he understood that the gentleman who censored the article, knowing that there were no kings present on the occasion, thought it would be wrong to say that any of them had departed. The war correspondents at the time were liberal in their use of quotations and not infrequently seemed to get into trouble with the censor as a result. On another occasion a man from _The Times_ quoted from Browning during a description of the shelling of the Germans at Hulluch. The lines he chose:

Twenty-nine distinct damnations,
   One sure, if the other fails.

ran foul of the military censor at the front, who

deleted 'Twenty-nine distinct' and substituted 'different'. The Home Secretary, again put on the spot in the House of Commons, was once more candid in his reply. The alteration was not due to any objection by the censors to the poets, he said, but to their failure to recognise them. _The Times_ itself was moved to comment on the incidents. 'Is it conceivable,' the newspaper asked in its rhetorical way, 'that the censors number two such idiots in their ranks?' _The Times_ also revealed that a military censor at the front had been at work on a report sent to them by John Buchan, the novelist, describing the Battle of Loos in September 1915. During the course of his dispatch Buchan had described the desperate valour shown by the German troops, but this passage was excised. The matter was raised in the House of Commons, when the Home Secretary said that the sentences appeared in a section of the article which the censor decided had to be removed because it contained information that might have been of value to the enemy. The House maintained, however, that the censor's treatment of the passage showed that his first intention had been to cut out the favourable references to the enemy and that was certainly the view held by John Buchan, who later referred to the incident in a lecture given on his return home. Nothing could be more grossly unjust or unfounded, he said, than to suggest that the

British were unwilling to admit good qualities in their enemies. He added that British soldiers were noted for their generous admiration of the soldierly qualities of their enemies. There were certainly many examples of this from the western front during the war and Michael MacDonagh was a witness, nearer home, of the camaraderie that sometimes spontaneously broke out between the combatant rank and file. He was at Clapham Junction one day when two special trains drew up at opposite sides of the same station. One carried dishevelled German prisoners brought straight from the battlefields of Flanders. The other was packed with young British soldiers, new recruits on their way to the front for the first time. The Germans smiled, waved and called out *Kamerad!* The British shouted 'Good old Jerries', and threw packets of chocolate and tobacco to the Germans.

Concern to control the news derived partly from the flood of rumour, suspicion and alarm that ran through the country in the early months of war, and which fed anti-German sentiment. The Press was full of atrocity stories. One notorious report in a Scottish newspaper alleged that a young nurse in a Belgian hospital had had both her breasts cut off by the Germans; others reported the raping of nuns, mutilation of young girls, and the impaling of babies on German bayonets. Some of the most persistent — if unlikely — of such rumours were the published and unpublished reports of Russian troops ('little

German reservists living in England were arrested shortly after war was declared when trying to cross to the Continent. They were marched under guard through Folkestone to Shorncliffe Camp. 69

As soon as war was declared many Germans living in Britain were arrested by the police. In London some 300 were taken to Olympia, the stadium used only a few weeks earlier for the International Horse Show. It was made clear by the Home Office that the wholesale detention of Germans was only a precautionary measure. 70

69

short of a million', according to a reporter from *The Times*) who were seen to have landed in Aberdeen early in September 1914 with 'snow on their boots', and were said to have passed through England on their way to reinforce the western front. The reports were fed by many, apparently authentic, eye-witness accounts. Trains were reported travelling south with the blinds down, station slot-machines were jammed with roubles, porters were seen sweeping snow from railway carriages, and when the trains stopped at Carlisle there was an unprecedented demand for vodka and coffee. Michael MacDonagh was one of those who helped to spread the rumour. He confessed that, like everybody else, he 'kept the ball a-rolling', the only excuse that could be offered being that it was a 'case of the wish

being father to the thought'. On 15 September the Press Bureau issued an absolute denial of the rumour, having apparently let it run for a week or two in the hope that it might be believed by the Germans and help boost morale at home. How the rumour originated has never been satisfactorily explained, though MacDonagh attributed it to a telegram received by a wholesale dealer of provisions in London. The telegram read: 'Two hundred thousand Russians being dispatched via Archangel.' The reference proved to be not to troops, but to eggs.

Atrocity stories and the spy fever which gripped the country at the beginning of the war led to suspicion of anyone with a German-sounding name, and sometimes to more than suspicion. Attacks in

71

The Globe and some other newspapers forced the resignation of Prince Louis of Battenberg, the First Sea Lord and a cousin of the King, who had been a naturalised Briton for more than forty years. The King noted the occasion in his diary for 29 October 1914: 'Saw Winston Churchill who informed me that Louis of Battenberg had resigned his appt. as 1st Sea Lord. The Press & Public have said so many things against him being born a German, & that he ought not to be at the head of the Navy, that it was best for him to go. I feel deeply for him: there is no more loyal man in the country.' The King himself was not immune to popular pressure. Against his wishes he was persuaded to the dropping of the names of the German Emperor and his son from the British Army List and to the removal of eight enemy Knights of the Garter from the Order as well as taking down their banners from St George's Chapel at Windsor. The King's sensitivity to criticism (he was told that it was whispered that he must be pro-German since he and his family had German names) led him, in 1917, to change his name. Many new possibilities were suggested, including Tudor-Stewart, Plantagenet, York, Lancaster, and Eng-

Vice-Admiral Prince Louis of Battenberg, First Sea Lord, who was forced to resign because, though a naturalised Briton for more than forty years, he had been born a German. 71

The sinking of the liner *Lusitania* by a German submarine in 1915, with the loss of more than 1,000 lives, stimulated much anti-German feeling in Britain. An artist's impression of the liner going down, from *The Illustrated London News* of 15 May 1915, and a photograph of the liner's dining saloon. 72, 73

land, but in the end the name Windsor, suggested by Lord Stamfordham, the King's Private Secretary, was chosen and announced, on 18 July, in the following terms:

'We, of Our Royal Will and Authority, do hereby declare and announce that as from the date of this Our Royal Proclamation Our House and Family shall be styled and known as the House and Family of Windsor, and that all the descendants in the male line of Our said Grandmother Queen Victoria who are subjects of these Realms, other than female

descendants who may marry or may have married, shall bear the said Name of Windsor:

'And do hereby further declare and announce that We for Ourselves and for and on behalf of Our descendants and all other descendants of Our said Grandmother Queen Victoria who are subjects of these Realms, relinquish and enjoin the discontinuance of the use of the degrees, styles, dignities, titles and honours of Dukes and Duchesses of Saxony and Princes and Princesses of Saxe-Coburg and Gotha, and all other German degrees, styles, dignitaries, titles, honours and appellations to Us or to them heretofore belonging or appertaining.'

The anti-German crusade also had its effects lower down the social order. *The Daily Mail* carried prominent warnings to its readers about being served by Austrian or German waiters. 'If your waiter says he is Swiss,' the newspaper cautioned, 'ask to see his passport.' *The National Review* launched a campaign against aliens in the City of London, one of its targets being Sir Edgar Speyer, the chairman of the London Underground and member of a family firm with offices also in New York and Frankfurt. As he had a house on the

Norfolk coast it was rumoured that he signalled to U-boats from his garden. An attempt was made to force him out of the Privy Council, of which he was a member, and though this failed he left the country and his name was removed from the Privy Council after the war. In 1915 all German music was banned from orchestral concerts, but the boycott of such composers as Beethoven and Wagner did not last long. The torpedoing of the liner *Lusitania* by a U-boat off the Irish coast, with the loss of more than 1,000 lives, further stimulated anti-German passions in 1915. German shops were attacked and looted in the East End of London and German pianos were thrown into the street. The internment of all Germans was demanded. In fact 19,000 had already been interned, but in response to the agitation the Prime Minister announced that all male aliens still free would be interned or, if over military age, would be repatriated along with women and children.

At home the Defence of the Realm Act was occasionally used at first to try to protect the public from the knowledge that this war would involve the civilian as well as the man at the front. Detailed reports

74

75

Anti-German rioting after the sinking of the *Lusitania*. At Poplar, in east London, a shop, believed to be owned by Germans, was looted. In Liverpool a German butcher shop was wrecked by angry demonstrators. 74, 75

Three towns on the east coast — Scarborough, Whitby and Hartlepool — were bombarded by German cruisers in December 1914. Some fifty people were killed. The drawing shows the damage caused by a shell which struck a Baptist chapel in Hartlepool. 76

of the first live action on the home front were not immediately published but when they were made public indignation was such that the authorities quickly appreciated the psychological and propaganda advantages in letting people know that they too were involved in 'total war'. In any case there was no effective means of censoring news of coastal bombardments and Zeppelin raids though the Press still had to print the 'official' accounts put out by the Press Bureau. The first realisation that the war would have to be fought at home as well as abroad

76

came on 16 December 1914 when German cruisers made a sortie into the North Sea and bombarded Scarborough, Whitby and Hartlepool. About fifty civilians were killed, including women and children, the Grand Hotel at Scarborough was wrecked and the ruins of Whitby Abbey suffered further damage. The raid caused a sensation, vividly recorded by Mrs Peel: 'The newspapers, which until then had been full of photographs of the war at the front, were now filled with "scenes of the English bombard-ment". It seemed incredible that an English girl at Scarborough should be killed by a German whilst cleaning the doorstep! That a British family of eight at Hartlepool should every one of them be slaughtered by Germans! When the wreckage was removed from the home of these unfortunates the dog and the canary were found crushed, but the cat, the only living thing to escape, was sleeping unharmed beneath the washing copper. And what a heroine was the milk-girl going on her rounds with

77

78

Air raid damage at Yarmouth on the night of 19 January 1915.   77

The Zeppelin, a large and cumbersome machine capable of carrying only a very small bomb-load, could not be rated highly as a weapon of war, though it was rather more effective as a means of intimidation. Once the Zeppelin raids began, in 1915, it quickly became evident that Britain's air defences were inadequate, even against such a vulnerable object as the airship.   78

A hastily erected searchlight, part of the coastal anti-aircraft defences.   79

Advertisement based on the recognition of the importance of the Royal Flying Corps.   80

80

79

the breakfast milk whose hat was hit though she escaped unhurt.... Ten thousand sightseers visited Scarborough to see with their own eyes the almost unbelievable wreckage of an English town by the guns of German ships, and the publicity given resulted in a great rush of recruits.'

The first air raid on Britain took place over the Christmas holiday in 1914 when a solitary aircraft dropped a bomb on Dover. It fell in a garden, and the only damage resulting from its explosion was the breaking of a few windows. On the following day another German aircraft flew over the Thames Estuary and dropped a bomb near a village in Kent, again causing only small damage. These incidents caused little excitement compared with the coastal bombardments, or compared with the Zeppelin raids which began in the following year.

The Zeppelin was a large, slow and cumbersome machine, 600 feet long or more, yet, notwithstanding its size, it could carry only a small amount of bombs weighing merely a few pounds each, and these could not be dropped with any accuracy. As a weapon of war it could not be rated very highly, but as a machine of hostile intent flying high over the English countryside, towns and cities, it was both fascinating and terrifying. It was therefore of some significance as a means of intimidation, particularly when it was first used in 1915, since the defences were acknowledged to be inadequate to meet them. The Admiralty was responsible for air defence at this time and Winston Churchill gave an account to the War Council early in the year of what these defences were, as recorded in the Cabinet Papers:

'The moment a hostile airship was sighted the

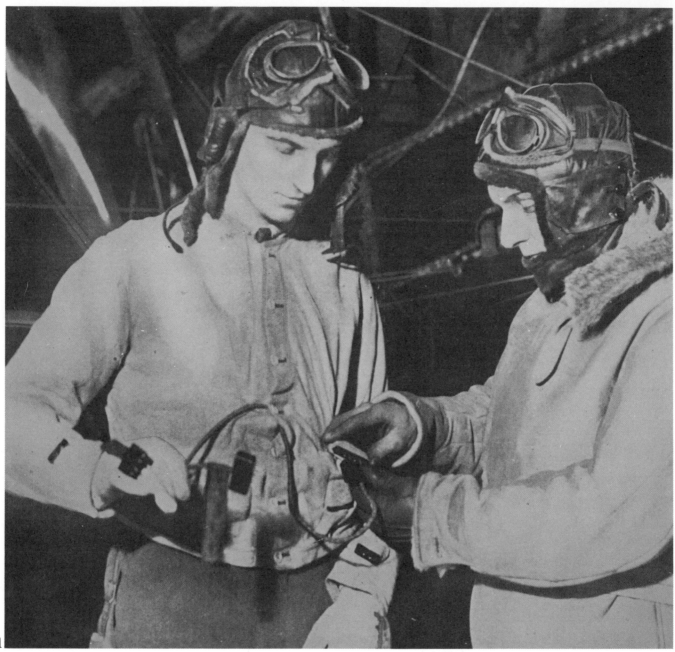

81

Electrically-heated clothing for airmen flying in cold weather was introduced early in the war, though the censor did not allow this photograph to be published until 1918.   81

alarm would be given and the aeroplanes would ascend. Those on the coast would probably not be able to rise sufficiently high to attack the airships on their approach, but would be ready for them on their return; those at Hendon, however, should be ready to attack the airships as they neared London. These aeroplanes were armed with rifles firing incendiary bullets, which, in the course of experiments, had proved their capacity to destroy a balloon. In addition, he believed that some flyers were prepared to charge a Zeppelin. Within the same triangle there are nine three-inch, thirty-nine 6-pounders, and twenty-eight pompom guns — a total of seventy-six anti-aircraft guns. In London itself there are two three-inch, four six-pounders, and five pompoms, with thirteen searchlights. The three-inch is a powerful and accurate long-range gun. The pompoms were now being provided with incendiary shell.'

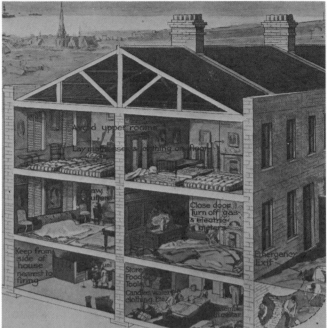

82

Air and sea raid precautions issued early in the war advised householders to avoid rooms at the top of the house, to put mattresses and clothing on the floors of the upper rooms, to turn off gas and electricity, to keep away from the side of the house 'nearest to the firing', and to ensure that there was an emergency escape from the cellar.   82

Queen Mary inspecting firemen and firewomen at an explosives factory.   83

In spite of these defences Churchill conceded that the Zeppelin would still get through. 'If the enemy thought it worthwhile to attack London merely for the purpose of injuring and terrorising the civil population and damaging property, there was no means of preventing it. In order to reduce the loss of life to a minimum, instructions had been published by the police warning the populace to remain indoors. The Fire Brigade had worked out careful plans for meeting a simultaneous outbreak of a number of fires.'

Sir Charles Petrie, who was later to become a regular contributor to *The Illustrated London News*, spent the early part of the war serving with an anti-aircraft battery at Shoeburyness in the Thames Estuary. In his memoirs, *A Historian Looks at his World*, he has left an account of their state of preparation which would certainly have been disquieting if it had been published then. 'We were trained on a variety of guns, both fixed and mobile, and there were not a few accidents owing to the different lengths of recoil.... The only time a Zeppelin came within range we had no ammunition and were constrained to admire her beauty in the moonlight; perhaps, however, the lack of shells did not matter so much as we imagined at the time, for when they did arrive they were filled with nothing more deadly than salt. Indeed, the position of many gun stations seemed to be dictated by political rather than military considerations. Lack of ammunition was the rule rather than the exception, but all the

83

Anti-aircraft guns forming part of Britain's coastal defences. One of the crew on a site in the Thames Estuary reported after the war that the only time a Zeppelin came in range 'we had no ammunition, and were constrained to admire her beauty in the moonlight'. 84, 85

same officers and men had to pretend that the guns were ready for action, presumably to impress the civilian population, and each night we were compelled to stand by as if we were in a position to open fire. It was a sorry and somewhat demoralising piece of make-believe.'

Nonetheless London made what preparations it could. Steel nets were draped over some of the more important public buildings, including Buckingham Palace and the War Office, with the object of deflecting bombs, and the five-acre lake in St James's Park was drained so that it would not serve as an identification point from the air for the many buildings of official London that surrounded it. A hutted encampment spread across its dry bed, with offices of the Mercantile Marine on one side of the bridge and those of departments anxious to prevent trade with the enemy on the other.

The Zeppelins began their raids soon after the Kaiser signed the necessary order in February 1915. In spite of the advice of Winston Churchill and the Admiralty, and the police warnings to the populace to remain indoors, curiosity generally got the better of caution. One woman recalled hearing an odd 'chunketty, chunketty' noise one day, 'as if a train with rusty wheels were travelling through the sky'. Inevitably, like almost everyone else who heard the noise, she ran to see what it was, and saw her first Zeppelin. Michael MacDonagh recorded a similar experience. Writing in his study one night shortly before eleven o'clock, he was disturbed by the roar of bombs and guns. Stepping outside he saw an amazing spectacle: 'High in the sky was a Zeppelin picked out of the darkness by searchlights — a long narrow object of a silvery hue. I felt like a watcher of the skies must feel when a new planet swims into his ken. For it was my first sight of an enemy airship!' On the following morning MacDonagh went out to survey the damage. He found gutted and smouldering warehouses in Wood Street and Silver Street, behind Cheapside and quite close to Guildhall, and near Liverpool Street station he found the site where a bomb had dropped near a

meagre official reports of such incidents he found the Press Bureau's explanation convincing. 'The Zeppelins attack under cover of moonless and dark nights. Landmarks cannot be identified by them. In their official reports published in the German newspapers they say they have dropped bombs on places of military importance which, in fact, they have never been near. Why should we enlighten them? Our desire is to keep the enemy in the dark, and we can do that only by keeping the people also in the dark.'

The people of London, however, did not wish to be kept in the dark. Whenever a Zeppelin came over the city they assembled in the streets to watch it and they were more than ready to enjoy the spectacle when, in the autumn of 1916, the pilots of the Royal Flying Corps at last started to shoot them down. The first airship to be brought down on British soil, the L21, fell at Cuffley, in Hertfordshire, at 3 a.m. on 3 September 1916. In spite of the hour large crowds had poured into the streets of London to watch and cheer when Lt. William Leefe Robinson (who won the Victoria Cross for his deed) shot the airship down. As the Zeppelin burst into flames a great cry went up as if, *The Spectator* suggested, a goal had been nobly won in a football match. Another lone spectator said it sounded as if a far-away London was cheering: 'Almost unconsciously I began to cry

Mr Alfred de Rothschild's house in Mayfair, as well as more important public buildings, was protected by steel wiring which it was hoped was strong enough to explode a falling bomb before it hit the roof.   86

The first Zeppelin to be brought down on British soil fell at Cuffley in Hertfordshire, on 3 September 1916. It was shot down by a fighter pilot, and its slow descent to earth after it had burst into flames was watched by thousands. Vast crowds of sightseers and souvenir-hunters swarmed into Cuffley on the following day.   87

bus, killing the driver and nine passengers. Thirty-eight people were killed and 124 injured in this raid, but neither MacDonagh nor any other reporter was allowed to publish his own account. Instead a brief report was put out by the Press Bureau, stating simply that 'a London district' was 'visited', and that incendiary and explosive bombs were dropped. The stereotyped official descriptions of such raids as 'visits' were the cause of much scornful laughter, MacDonagh noted, but on investigation of the

88

89

The remains of two Zeppelins shot down over Essex in September 1916.   88, 89

"Hooray! hooray!" too, but suddenly I stopped. We were cheering whilst men who were after all very bravely doing what they thought it their duty to do were being burned to death.' For the rest of that day — a Sunday — Cuffley was the centre of vast crowds of sightseers and souvenir-hunters, only comparable — as many observed at the time — with the excited crowds of Derby Day.

Three more Zeppelins were brought down within a month, and each with similar popular rejoicing. Two — the L33 and the L32 — were shot down on 23 September, one at Wigborough and one at Billericay. The third, the L31, after crossing London, was blown up over Potters Bar in Hertfordshire on the night of 1 October. It was witnessed by Michael MacDonagh who noted that it was probably the most appalling spectacle associated with the war which London was likely to provide, its death being accompanied by 'a shout the like of which I never heard in London before — a hoarse shout of mingled execration, triumph and joy; a swelling shout that appeared to be rising from all parts of the metropolis, ever increasing in force and intensity'. The pilot of this Zeppelin, who had jumped from the airship before being burned alive like the rest of the crew, had hit the ground with such force that the imprint of his body was clearly marked in the earth. He was still alive when first found but died soon afterwards. His name, which was not published at the time, was Commander

Picked up in East Anglia, the observation car of a Zeppelin was later put on display in London.   90

The sinking of a Zeppelin witnessed by the crew of a Grimsby trawler.   91

After the Zeppelins came the aeroplanes. The first bombing raid on London by one of these machines took place in November 1916, and by the middle of the following year such raids had become commonplace. Londoners took temporary shelter wherever they could while the raiders were overhead, mainly in the doorways or basements of nearby buildings. 92

Victims of an air raid on a London school hit by bombs on the morning of 13 June 1917. 93

Heinrich Mathy, the most renowned of the German Zeppelin commanders.

After the Zeppelins, which were now regarded as much less of a threat, came the aeroplanes. The first bombing raid by one of these machines took place in daylight on 23 November 1916. Six bombs were dropped over central London, one of them hitting the Victoria Palace music-hall in Victoria Street, not far from Buckingham Palace. One of the largest raids took place on 25 May 1917 when twenty-four bombers crossed the Channel and headed for London. They were forced to scatter before reaching their target but dropped their bombs over the south-east of the country, killing nearly 100 people, many of them children. On 13 June another group of bombers reached London in a daylight raid, killing more than 150 people and seriously damaging railway stations. On 7 July a flight of twenty German aircraft again attacked London during daylight, killing fifty-seven and injuring 193. Michael MacDonagh was on his way to *The Times* when this raid took place. He recalled that when he saw the aircraft he was not disturbed for a moment by the thought that they might be German. 'The height at which they were flying was so low, their approach was so leisurely, and so well kept was their fan-like formation, that to suppose they were enemies was preposterous.' Nevertheless they were the enemy, and within minutes he was hearing the swish of their bombs and running to take cover in Blackfriars underground station.

The Central Telegraph Office was one of the buildings hit in this raid. The damage was slight, however, and none of the staff was hurt because they had gone down to the basement, having already received a warning of the raid in a telephone call from the War Office. It was the practice at that time to relay direct warnings of impending raids by telephone to selected vulnerable targets, but not to issue general warnings. This policy was criticised in a secret session debate in the House of Commons two days later. The Home Secretary, Sir George Cave, was asked why the Government persisted in its refusal to give the general public warning of an approaching raid. The answer given was that many

94

95

Following a bombing raid on the East End of London, homeless men carry their bedding to new accommodation.   94

An artist's impression of an anti-aircraft barrage of shrapnel shells bursting in the sky above Tower Bridge.   95

As a precaution against air raids, readers were advised to be ready to take their meals in their cellars.   96

warnings of such raids proved to be unfounded, and that if public warnings were given which were proved unnecessary people would, in time, come to disregard them. Such false alarms would involve stoppages of work which would interrupt produc-

tion in munition factories and other operations vital to the war effort. In spite of this the Government was, in the end, forced to introduce by popular pressure a system of warning by maroons. Lloyd George, who had become Prime Minister following Asquith's resignation in December 1916, attended the secret session in July and reported to the House that the Government hoped to reach soon so high a degree of equipment in aeroplanes that after the requirements of the Army in France were satisfied — still the first consideration — enough would be available for the defence of London. This would change the situation so completely that if the Germans came again they would get such a warm reception that they would deem it wiser, in future, to stay at home.

96

97

Meanwhile, people were left to take shelter as best they could when they found themselves in a raid. Underground stations, the crypts of churches and basements of large buildings were the places people made for if they were caught in the streets, either on foot or in buses or other vehicles and, when the moon was up, many people living in town centres would retreat to surrounding open spaces. The majority, however, determined to carry on as usual. *The Illustrated London News* published on 9 February 1918 this private letter (which had not been intended for publication) written by Miss Irene Miller, the novelist, as an example of how London carried on during an air raid:

'I couldn't send you a card last night to say we were all right, for long before the "All Clear" signal was given we were all in bed and sound asleep. The "All Clear" bugles just aroused me slightly, but only for half-a-second. I was dining at the Club when it commenced. The guns sounded very close, but nobody took any notice — nobody does now!

In the early days of air raids the Government would not issue public warnings of approaching raids because many might prove to be false alarms and would interrupt essential war work. Popular pressure, however, eventually forced the Government to introduce a system of warning by maroons, with subsequent 'All Clear' signs carried on vehicles or by Boy Scouts on bicycles. 97

Called *The Under World* and painted by Mr Walter Bayes, this picture of the Elephant and Castle tube station during an air raid was exhibited at the Royal Academy in 1918. It was described by *The Times* as having 'a sudden surprising tenderness in it', but by *The Pall Mall Gazette* as showing 'a wilful search for repulsive ugliness'. 98

The debris of a German 'Gotha' bomber, shot down over the sea, is hauled on board a British naval vessel. 99

98

The diners went on dining, the waiters went on waiting, and when it came to the speechifying, the speakers went on speaking — though I do think it must have been a bit of an ordeal to make a speech with that hubbub outside. It was a very nice little meal. First soup, and then an *entrée*, something "*à la belle Otero*", which was baked potato with the top cut off, the contents mashed and mixed with cut-up oysters, and put back again and re-baked for a few minutes. Then turkey — plenty of it, with potatoes and sprouts; then what they called an Italian pudding, made of a thin sort of macaroni with preserved cherries, very nice; and dessert.... It was a bit of a job to get home afterwards, for the raid was not officially over, though we had heard nothing of it for about an hour (it was twenty to twelve now). So I went in the Tube. There were a lot of people taking shelter there, sitting on the steps and platforms, but hundreds more were just going home in the ordinary way. The trains came along packed full, and they seemed to be running quite

frequently. Lots of those taking shelter weren't really terrified, I know, for they were loving couples, making it a sort of Hampstead Heath on Bank Holiday. Each soldier and his girl spread a newspaper on the platform, sat down, and leant against the wall, with their arms around each other's necks and their heads on each other's shoulders (so to speak). There were little groups of such, on the giggle, and enjoying themselves immensely; and, of course, Mother couldn't scold if one stayed out with one's best boy, and explained that it was all the Air Raid, *could* she? The firing recommenced very noisily after a while; and there were quite a lot of people out, but nobody took any notice, and when I got home the family were all comfortably in bed.'

The letter was quoted in the 'Ladies' Page' of the magazine, and its regular contributor, who signed herself 'Filomena', accompanied it with a fine example of the then fashionable purple prose on the subject of the air raids:

'Fine, heartening, but absolutely lying tales are cheering the spiteful enemy about the terror inspired in Londoners by air-raids. The hideous German natures, believing themselves safe from reprisals by reason of our incapacity, moral or physical, for such retaliation, chortle in their glee, less at the idea of the babes murdered in their cradles, the quiet civilians, and the gentle women maimed or killed, than at the silly notion of our universal fright. Not

100

In 1915 the Ministry of Munitions was set up with Mr David Lloyd George at its head. By the end of the war the Ministry was responsible for the direction of some three million workers, and had provided the impetus for the introduction of many regulations governing the behaviour of British citizens.　100

A shell factory in the east end of London and a training class for munitions workers run by the London County Council.　101, 102

so much at the thought of a hundred or two killed and wounded do they rejoice as at the sweet vision they evoke of all London rushing into dank cellars, and all our ordinary life abruptly stopped by our millionfold fears. Far, far otherwise, O Hun! is the truth. The crowd that does rush for shelter is in a microscopic proportion composed of the still absurdly large alien population in our Metropolis. English mothers very properly seek shelter and safety for their children; but the average, the common or garden Englishman and Englishwoman, displays a cool, calm courage that is really remarkable. Very keen regret is in many hearts the while, but panic terror — a complete stop in life's business to hurry to shelter — not a bit of it. You flatter yourselves, O Huns!, in this foul notion.'

101

102

The air raids continued into the last year of the war, some of the most persistent and fierce occurring at night in January and February 1918. Forty-seven people were killed and 169 injured on the night of 29 January. A direct hit on the Odhams printing works in Long Acre, Covent Garden, caused the deaths of thirty-eight people sheltering in the basement. On that night, for the first time, an 'apron screen' of balloons secured to steel cables was used to help in the air defences of London and one of the German 'Gotha' bombers was shot down. But though the air defences of the country became stronger they were never given the priority of the western front, and two squadrons of aircraft withdrawn from France to help with the defence of Britain were soon returned at the insistence of the commanders in the field. Furthermore, despite the alarms and concern the air raids caused, their damage, in comparison with what happened in the Second World War, was slight and their influence on the course of the war negligible. A total of 1,117 civilians lost their lives as a result of the Zeppelin and aircraft bombing raids and some 3,000 were injured.

In addition to such direct, uncomfortable and

unexpected involvement in the war the ordinary citizen found his life becoming more and more regulated — and generally in the cause of the defence of the realm. Much of the initial impetus came from the setting up of the Ministry of Munitions under Lloyd George. Created in 1915 with no staff and using a requisitioned hotel as offices, it had, by the end of the war, amassed a staff of more than 60,000 and was responsible for the direction of some three million industrial workers. The Government had assumed powers to requisition raw materials, which the Ministry of Munitions did in the case of steel. Under the Munitions of War Act of 1915 the Government also took authority to deal with industrial stoppages and to assume direct control of key factories, in which normal trade union activities were forbidden. Strikes or resistance to 'dilution' (the use of unskilled workers and women) in the munitions industry became illegal. A War Munitions Volunteer Scheme was brought in, under which the Government had power to direct workers who joined it and tribunals were set up to deal with infringements.

Such actions were resisted by the Labour movement. In July 1915 the miners of South Wales

Destroyer under construction in a naval ship-building yard, and the Prince of Wales working a pneumatic riveting hammer during a visit to a Clyde shipyard during 1918.   103, 104

went on strike to enforce the closed shop. Though some members of the Government wished to use the powers of the law the strike was resolved by conciliation — Lloyd George virtually agreeing to all the miners' demands. Later in the year there was serious opposition by industrial workers in Glasgow to dilution and other measures designed to reduce restrictive practices in their work. Lloyd George went up to Glasgow on Christmas Day to meet a large gathering of shop stewards. He was given a rowdy reception. The socialist journal *Forward* began its report of the occasion: 'The best paid munitions worker in Britain, Mr Lloyd George (almost £100 a week), visited the Clyde last week in search of adventure. He got it.' *Forward* was

suppressed for its report though in essence it seems to have been an accurate account. Lloyd George was, in fact, howled down and was unable to deliver his speech. The official version of the occasion, as recounted by the Press Bureau, made no reference to the disturbances nor to the fact that the speech was not delivered. In this incident the law was brought in and David Kirkwood, the chief shop steward, was deported to Edinburgh, although he was later brought back. The Ministry of Munitions did not again attempt to use its legal powers in this area and there were no serious strikes among the factories of Glasgow during the rest of the war.

The Defence of the Realm regulations also embraced attempts to defend citizens against themselves — the most notorious being the official moves to control the nation's drinking habits. Lloyd George took the lead in the campaign to reduce the national consumption of alcohol, which he believed to be seriously affecting productivity. 'We are fighting Germans, Austrians and Drink,' he said in

1915, 'and so far as I can see the greatest of these deadly foes is Drink.' Full employment and high wages were, Lloyd George believed, leading to increased drinking among the working classes. Public houses, which were open from early morning until midnight, were often visited by labourers on their way to work, as well as after work, and Lloyd George was able to find plenty of examples of urgent war work apparently held up by the difficulty of getting men out of the pubs or of getting them to work on time after a heavy night's drinking. Armed with these examples, and with the precedents of France and Russia, whose governments had prohibited the sale of absinthe and vodka, Lloyd George embarked on a crusade. In such a mood, as Harold

Nicolson noted in his biography of King George V, Lloyd George was irresistible, and his first victim was the King himself. 'On March 29, 1915,' wrote Nicolson, 'he bustled into the King's audience room, his little arms swinging with excitement, his eyes flashing flame, his lower lip protruding with scorn of those who drank.' The King was affected by his enthusiasm, and offered to set an example to the nation by giving up all alcoholic liquor and to issue orders against its consumption in the Royal Household. The offer was accepted and on 6 April it was announced that no alcohol would be absorbed by the Royal Family or Household. The King wrote in his diary: 'This morning we have all become teetotaller until the end of the war. I have done it as

104

an example, as there is a lot of drinking going on in the country at large, so other measures had to be good.' But the 'King's Pledge' was not an example that was widely followed, not even by some of the senior members of the Cabinet, and certainly not by the country at large, so other measures had to be resorted to. One was the introduction of a 'No Treating' order designed to curtail the standing of drinks to soldiers and the buying of rounds. Under these regulations any drink ordered had to be paid for by the person supplied with the drink. A number of husbands were fined for buying their wives a drink but the evident absurdities of the regulation were justified in the eyes of the legislators by the fact

In July 1915 the miners of South Wales defied wartime regulations and went on strike to try to enforce the closed shop. Though some members of the Government wanted to use the law to break the strike it was ultimately ended by conciliation. 105

The Minister for Munitions and soon to be Prime Minister, Mr Lloyd George at work in his office in 1915. 106

that there was a fall in the consumption of alcohol. Other rules prohibited the purchase of drinks 'on the slate' and curtailed the licensing hours. In London, for example, the new opening hours were from noon to 2.30 p.m. and from 6.30 p.m. to 9.30 p.m. whereas before November 1915 they had been 5 a.m. to half an hour after midnight. As a final shot in the campaign against alcoholism the beer was watered. The effect of these measures was statistically impressive; convictions for drunkenness fell by about seventy-five per cent between 1914 and 1918 and the nation's consumption of alcohol fell by some fifty per cent in the same period.

The Defence of the Realm Act spread the wings of authority in many other directions as the war progressed. Rents were pegged to their 1914 level. Price control was enforced for milk. The owners of homing pigeons had to be registered. Londoners were not allowed to whistle for cabs. People were forbidden to loiter near railway bridges or tunnels, could not buy binoculars without official authorisation, nor fly a kite that might be used for signalling. Stiff fines were imposed for showing lights at night. A 'Curfew Order' restricted late-night activities by

105

forcing public restaurants and hotels to switch their dining room lights out at 10 p.m., and all theatres and other places of amusement to end their performances not later than 10.30 p.m. Although such restrictions were aggravating, the reasons were in general understood and accepted. Most Britons would probably have agreed with G.K. Chesterton, who wrote in his column one week in 1917 that 'before we begin complaining of the inconveniences which now necessarily entangle us, it would be well to remember that there are many, both friends and foes, who wish (like the cabman contemplating the drunken gentleman) that they had half our complaint. For indeed, our very reasons for complaint are reasons for contentment.' Chesterton's point was that, in spite of current difficulties, the inhabitant of Balham was still better off than the inhabitant of Belgium. 'It should be remembered,' Chesterton concluded, 'that, though the enemy has not yet suffered anything proportionate to his crimes, or anything equivalent to the sufferings of his victims, he is already suffering far more than we are, in the special fashion in which we are.... Under his Defence of the Realm Act there is not so much a restraint of liberty as no liberty to be restrained. It is a master of slaves that he would win, if he did win; it is as a master of slaves that he will fall, when he does fall.'

4 WOMEN AT WORK

The advent of war brought an immediate truce in the fight for women's suffrage. Mrs Emmeline Pankhurst steered the extremist Women's Social and Political Union into intense nationalist support for the war and the Suffragists took a leading part in campaigning, in the early stages of the war, for women's services to be effectively made use of. This was a demand that the Government and many individual employers, including farmers, were reluctant to concede. The first attempts by women to organise themselves for war effort met not only official reserve, but also sometimes outright rebuff. Dr Elsie Inglis, a Scottish medical practitioner who offered to form a women's ambulance unit, was turned away from the War Office with the words: 'My good lady, go home and sit still.' She refused to follow this advice and set up Scottish women's hospitals in France and the Balkans. Filomena, in her column on the 'Ladies' Page' of *The Illustrated London News*, was quick to reflect the exasperation felt by many women at the general reluctance to give them worthwhile employment. 'So many of us are *aching* to do something,' she wrote, 'to do our bit for England, and we find official coldness, indifference, polite gibes, inadequate effort to understand and accept all that women can do in the national emergency.' Mrs Peel recorded the case of one woman, typical of many, who was made thoroughly miserable because no one seemed to want her. Wherever she applied there were already great numbers of women waiting for jobs. Eventually she found work in the packing department of a hospital stores workroom, where she stood for hours each day wrestling with coarse string and sacking which made her hands painfully sore. 'I was very stupid about getting the corners neat and I got dreadfully tired,' she subsequently recalled, 'but I was so thankful to be doing something to help.' In March 1915 the Board of Trade, responding partly to the pressure of the women themselves and partly to the needs of the times, appealed to all women prepared to take paid employment of any kind, in trade, commerce or agriculture, to put their names on the Register of Women for War Service. 'If the full fighting power of the Nation is to be put forth on the field of battle,' the Board of Trade declared, 'the full working power of the Nation must be available to carry on its ordinary processes at home. Any woman who by working helps to release and equip a man for

107

The war brought an abrupt end to the militant campaign for women's suffrage and Mrs Emmeline Pankhurst, here seen being arrested and removed from the railings in front of Buckingham Palace in May 1914, led her suffrage movement into the organisation of women for war work.   107

fighting does national war service.'

Londoners had already noted that women were beginning to substitute for men in occupations previously exclusively filled by males. Women were acting as lift attendants in the big stores, were driving delivery vans and had been taken on as waiters in some of the London clubs, including the Athenaeum. But such activities were peripheral and certainly did not satisfy women's demand to be given work that more directly helped the war effort.

109

Three months after the appeal to women to register was made it was noted that only some 1,400 of more than 80,000 who had put down their names had been found jobs. Filomena commented again on the situation in her column on 15 May:

'"Here is a recruiting sergeant," I said to the young woman who was walking with me; "see the little bunch of ribbons on his cap." To which she replied, with a heavy, longing sigh, "He should recruit me if he might." Thousands of girls, beyond

Theatre call-boys having joined Kitchener's Army, their place was taken by women and girls. At the Shaftesbury Theatre in 1915, where *The Arcadians* was playing, the cast was summoned to the stage by this fourteen-year-old girl.   108

The British School of Motoring urged women to learn to drive not only because it was 'healthy, enjoyable and highly remunerative', but also because of the great need for women drivers.   109

Billposting was another occupation in which women substituted for men.   110

111

a doubt, are in a similar frame of mind. It is hard indeed for them to realise that they may be filling a niche where their work is as important as going to the front. Yet any sort of chance to render self-devotion to the Motherland would be gladly grasped by a great number of strong, energetic young women, and possibly they might be employed in active war service of more than one kind in far greater numbers than has yet been thought of. They might be stretcher-bearers at the front, and orderlies, for instance, to set free many of the thousands of men engaged in such perilous but non-combatant work. The happy chance has, in fact, come to a few women, and has been splendidly met, apparently, by all to whom it has been fortunately allowed by fate. Major Gordon, who acts continuously as King's Messenger between our King and the Belgian hero-King, told the St John's Ambulance Association recently of the good work being done at the front by Lady Dorothy Feilding and many others. One incident, he said, had filled him with admiration and amazement. In one of the towns still held by the Belgian Army, and constantly shelled, so that the streets are most unsafe, Major Gordon saw an ambulance wagon coolly driven in by an English girl; inside it were only two other British women. As calm as if on a tennis-court, these three picked up as many as the vehicle could take of wounded men, and drove off with their sad load to hospital. Thousands of girls' hearts will leap with

Recruited by the Post Office at Enfield, postwomen leave the sorting office to deliver the mail.   111

Bus conductresses in training were taken for a trial run to get them accustomed to the bus's motion. As well as collecting fares they had other duties to perform, for, as *The Illustrated London News* reported, in the thick London fogs of the time they had to run alongside the vehicle, guiding the driver with electric torches.   112

The wartime policewoman, from a painting by Higgins.   113

As ambulance drivers women won the highest praise, both at home and at the front, where a British major reported that they acted 'as calmly as if they were on a tennis-court'.   114

112

Higgin 113

114

Collecting the fares on the top deck of an Edinburgh tram. 115

Training for fire drill with the London Fire Brigade. 116

In the early years of the war women complained that they were not being given enough to do to help win the war. In July 1915 they expressed their concern by marching through the streets of London carrying banners which declared 'Women's Battle Cry is Work, Work, Work!' 117

Women workers attached to a veterinary hospital in London unload a forage van. 118

longing to go and do likewise as they read of this quiet heroism of their unnamed sisters, and they will feel damped and depressed if good housewifery be offered to them in exchange.'

Because of the initial difficulties of dilution most of the women who registered were given work in Government offices and in the clothing and leather trades. In Glasgow the municipal tramways took on two women conductors on a week's trial. The experiment was soon extended but in London the General Omnibus Company was not converted to the use of women for another nine months. In June 1915 *The Daily Mail* listed some of the 'new occupations' for women and included in its list tram conductors, lift attendants, shopwalkers, bookstall clerks, ticket collectors, motor-van drivers, milk deliverers, railway-carriage cleaners, window clean-

117

118

ers, dairy workers and shell-makers. The list was clearly aimed at middle-class women who had not previously worked, for many women of the lower classes had long been used to hard industrial labour, and it was mainly among the middle class that the agitation for work was now being generated. In July 1915 this agitation was concerted by Mrs Pankhurst into the form of a march through the streets of London. Some 30,000 women, supported by many bands, took part in the demonstration which took place in the pouring rain, and they carried banners demanding the right to work and serve. One of the most popular was 'Women's Battle Cry is Work, Work, Work', and another 'Shells made by a Wife may Save her Husband's Life'.

After watching the procession pass along the Embankment Lloyd George, as Minister of Munitions, received a deputation from Mrs Pankhurst who, as well as voicing the demand of women to be permitted to take part in war work, also put in a plea for wage conditions which would safeguard their standard of living and prevent them from being sweated or exploited by manufacturers. In his reply Lloyd George promised that women would be given a fair minimum wage for time work and the same rates for piece work as were paid to men. The problems of dilution and of overcoming

120

121

One bare-footed woman marched in the July 1915 parade representing a battle-scarred Belgium.   119

Preparing for work in the factories, women join in training at a London County Council technical class.   120

In a munitions factory, a woman at work on a machine making cartridge cases.   121

closed shop and other traditional restrictive practices made this a promise that was sometimes difficult to keep. Where the Government, however, had direct control the promise certainly was kept and Lloyd George was justified in declaring in his *War Memoirs* that the conditions for women workers established by the Ministry during the war had a permanent effect upon the status of women workers in this country. But it was not achieved without resistance. A number of trade unions objected to the entry of women into their fields of work on the grounds that it might reduce the standard of men's wages and farmers, though desperately short of labour, were for a long time reluctant to make use of women. And when women were employed they were not always paid the same rates for the job as men. In shell factories, for

122

Shell-making in the Vickers factory. By 1918 more than 900,000 women were working in the munitions industry.   122

The making of shells was uncomfortable and dangerous work, one of the hazards being toxic jaundice caused by TNT poisoning. The women who suffered were nicknamed 'canaries' because the jaundice turned their faces bright yellow.   123

The Women's Land Army was the first of the women's armies in the field.   124

example, the top weekly wage for men was £4 6s 6d, whereas for women it was £2 4s 6d. And at a factory in Croydon women who replaced men were paid 12s 6d, though some of the men they replaced had been earning £3. The munition girls were nicknamed munitionettes, and Mrs Peel recorded the comment of a male fitter, who described them as being 'smart as monkeys, but a bit too chatty'!

The demands for more and more men at the front and for the weapons and shells for them to fight with were unremitting and the number of women working continued to grow throughout the war. In

the munitions industry the number of working women increased by more than 100 per cent between July 1915 and July 1916 — from 256,000 to 520,000. By July 1917 the total was 819,000 and in 1918 it grew to more than 900,000. Many of these women were engaged in the making of shells — work which did not require much skill but which was monotonous, uncomfortable and dangerous. Lloyd George acknowledged, after the war, the difficulties they had had to face and the courage they had shown. 'They had to work under conditions of very real danger to life and limb,' he wrote, 'and what some of them probably dreaded still more, of grotesque disfigurement — for one of the perils which was associated with the shell-filling factories was toxic jaundice resulting from TNT poisoning. This ailment turned their faces a bright and repulsive yellow. The poor girls for this reason were nicknamed by their associates outside as "canaries". They were quite proud of this designation, for they had earned it in the path of duty.' There were 181 cases of this toxic jaundice in 1916, of which fifty-two resulted in death, 189 cases in 1917 (forty-four of them fatal), and thirty-four in 1918 (ten of them fatal).

Lloyd George also praised the courage of women working in a factory at Hayes to secure fuses in high-explosive shells. It was discovered that some American shells had a left-hand thread in one compartment which tended to unscrew as the shell rotated in flight, causing the shells to explode prematurely. To eliminate this the component part had to be stabbed in two places with a chisel to break the thread so that they would not unscrew. It was a risky task, for if a trace of the fulminate was ignited by the blow it would explode the shell; but it was one which the women cheerfully undertook. One morning several women in the factory were killed by such an explosion, but the rest went on working. Their forewoman, who before the war had been a lady's maid, told a Government representative that she was not going to run away, 'especially when I think of those poor boys in France who are facing more dangers than we are here'.

For women who wished to become even more directly involved in the war there came eventually the opportunity to join one of the women's services. The first of these 'armies' in the field was the Women's Land Army and the second was the Women's Royal Naval Service. The Navy, by any standards a conservative service, was surprisingly quick to make use of these new recruits. Wrens not only took over the role of cooks and clerks but became wireless telegraphists, writers, code experts, electricians, and performed many other unexpected tasks. Their Director ranked as an Admiral. The Army followed the Navy in February 1917, when the Women's Auxiliary Army Corps was formed and by the end of the war had recruited more than 39,000

125

126

As the war progressed, and more land was put under the plough, women replaced men in virtually all the labouring jobs on the farm.   125

The Women's Auxiliary Army Corps, here being used as an advertisement for raincoats, was formed in February 1917 and had recruited more than 39,000 women by the end of the war. Many of them served abroad. The WAAC chauffeur (right) trying to get the staff car under way was serving on the western front.   126, 127

women, of whom nearly 9,000 were serving abroad. Women were also recruited to assist the Royal Flying Corps, or Royal Air Force as it became in 1918, as clerks, fitters, drivers, cooks, storekeepers and similar occupations, and by the end of the war there were more than 9,000 women attached to the Air Force. Far more numerous than any of these services were the nursing services — the Red Cross, the St John's Ambulance Association, the Territorial Force Nursing Service and the Voluntary Aid Detachments (the VADs). They worked in hospitals at home, at or near the front in France or Germany and as far afield as East Africa and India. The voluntary workers among them were not always quickly or easily assimilated into the rigid routines imposed by highly-trained disciplinarian matrons, as has been most vividly described by Vera Brittain in *Testament of Youth*, but once at the front such niceties generally disappeared.

By the end of the war it was estimated that more than seven million women were at work in some

128

129

A roll-call of women drivers serving with the Royal Air Force.   128

Women at Buckingham Palace before receiving their decorations of the New Order of the British Empire, including the first class badge and star for Dame's Grand Cross. The new decoration was instituted by the King in June 1917.   129, 130

The nursing services — the Red Cross, the St John's Ambulance Association, the Territorial Force Nursing Service and the Voluntary Aid Detachments — worked in hospitals at home and in many overseas stations, including the front-line areas in France and Germany.   131

form or other. The largest proportionate increase in their employment occurred in transport (from 18,000 in 1914 to 117,000 in 1918), and the most dramatic (and probably the only) decline was in domestic service — from 1,658,000 to 1,258,000, a drop of 400,000. It was a substantial fall, a herald of things to come, but with more than a million still employed in domestic service at its end the war cannot be said to have destroyed the system.

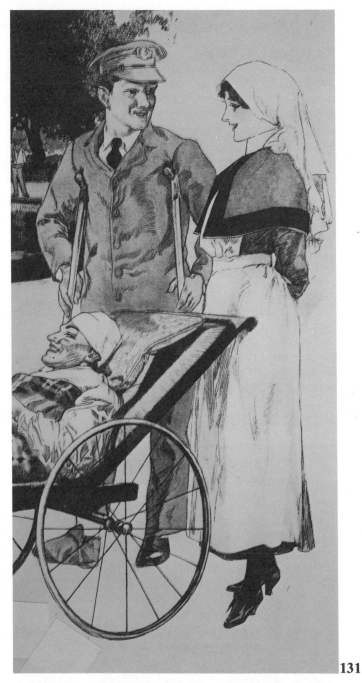

131

130

The courage and tenacity of so many women at work had its inevitable political reward in February 1918 when a Bill implementing the recommendations of the Speaker's conference that women should be given the vote was passed, without a division, in the House of Commons. Even so, the victory was not yet complete, for though women were declared to be qualified for election as MPs at the age of twenty-one they were only eligible to vote when they reached the age of thirty. This anomaly was not finally removed until 1927.

5 HARDSHIPS
AND ANNOYANCES

Lloyd George took office as Prime Minister on 7 December 1916, the political support for Asquith having collapsed because of the lack of direction that the war seemed to be receiving from the top. The difference between the two men was described by Lord Haldane: 'Asquith is a first-class head of a deliberative council. He is versed in precedents, acts on principle, and knows how and when to compromise. Lloyd George cares nothing for precedents and knows no principles, but he has fire in his belly and that is what we want.' Balfour commented: 'If he wants to be a dictator, let him be. If he thinks he can win the war, I'm all for his having a try.' The historian A.J.P. Taylor has suggested that Lloyd George was the nearest thing England has known to a Napoleon and that his accession to power was more than a change in government: it was a revolution, British-style. From the moment he came to power at the head of a new coalition the country was put into gear with one objective — winning the war. The effects of the change were described by the clerk of the Privy Council, Sir Almeric Fitzroy, as the 'substitution of dynamite for a damp squib'.

Lloyd George exercised his dynamite through a small war cabinet of only five members and by personal cunning, influence, inspiration and instinct. Five new departments of state were set up: shipping, labour, food, national service and food production, and within months the Government was able effectively to deploy a substantial machinery of state control. It did so with surprisingly little friction, largely because it was generally recognised that controls of this sort were necessary if the country was to have a chance of winning the war. The restrictions were nonetheless irksome and were sometimes accompanied by extraordinary antagonism — such as the case of the statutory introduction of daylight saving in May 1916. And such controversies were aggravated by increasing shortages of commodities such as coal, sugar, potatoes and margarine (butter was by this time virtually unobtainable). These shortages led in turn to the birth of that British phenomenon, the queue. The Government appointed a Food Controller and appealed to the public to eat less meat, pointing out that it was eaten two or three times a day by many people in the form of beef, mutton, pork or bacon. Shortly before Christmas 1916 an order for the regulation of meals was introduced, limiting lunches in hotels, restaurants, clubs and other public eating places to two courses, and dinners to three. That Christmas Filomena used her column in *The Illustrated London News* to extol the virtues of wholemeal bread which, she carefully explained, was more nutritious than the very white bread people were used to, and which she thought habit would soon render palatable. She also warned her readers of the need for economy in eating:

'Instead of the happy old-time considerations of how to honour Christmas with feasting, we have to signal this year's sad anniversary of the advent of the Prince of Peace by learning to lessen every

The British tradition of the queue developed from the shortages of the First World War. On Hammersmith Broadway the long bus queues were kept in order by special constables. 132

In December 1916 the Asquith Government collapsed and a new administration under Mr David Lloyd George took charge of the conduct of the war. The change was described at the time as the 'substitution of dynamite for a damp squib'! 133

132

THE NEW WAR MINISTRY.

Lord Curzon *Hoppe*
Lord President of the Council

Lord Milner *Vandyk*
Without portfolio

Mr. A. Henderson *Lafayette*
Without portfolio

Mr. Lloyd George *Vandyk*
Prime Minister

Mr. Bonar Law *Lafayette*
Chancellor of the Exchequer

Lord Devonport *Elliott & Fry*
Food Controller

Dr. Addison *Russell*
Minister of Munitions

Lord Derby *Russell*
Secretary for War

Lord Rhondda *Elliott & Fry*
Local Government Board

Sir Albert Stanley *Elliott & Fry*
President of the Board of Trade

Sir George Cave *Lafayette*
Home Secretary

Sir Edward Carson *Russell*
First Lord of the Admiralty

Lord Robert Cecil *Elliott & Fry*
Minister of Blockade

Sir Robert Finlay *Elliott & Fry*
Lord Chancellor

133

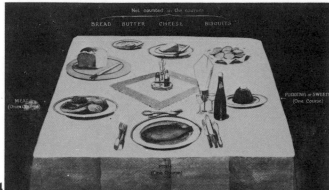

134

135

In 1916 the Government imposed restrictions on the size of meals served in hotels, restaurants, clubs and other public eating places. A maximum of two courses was allowed for lunch, and three for dinner. A sample of the 'New War Dinner', as published at the time, is shown here.   134

Communal kitchens were set up to help cope with food shortages. The soup and meat pies were particularly recommended by the magazines of the day.   135

A Bovril advertisement drawing attention to the need for everyone to cut down on their food intake by at least one-fifth.   136

An offer from the British Commercial Gas Association to help with the management of small households.   137

A cartoon from *The Sketch* of February 1917, captioned 'The Fashionable Complaint: Growing Pains'!   138

The Food Question

family's consumption of food. We must *all* realise the extreme and immediate necessity of food economy. It is not a mere question of whether any individual can afford to pay at present whatever money may be asked for food. We must try to visualise all the food in the country as one stock, to be consumed as carefully as possible by everybody, in order that it may last out and that all of us of every class may have sufficient as long as possible.'

The Board of Agriculture was authorised to take possession of unoccupied land and also to use portions of commons and parks for the growing of food. Thus began the 'allotment' system. All

WE must all cut down our food by at least one-fifth, but at the same time we must preserve our health and power to win the war. Fortunately there is one food substance which enables us to eat less and yet obtain the same amount of nourishment. That food is Bovril.

"The addition of a small teaspoonful of Bovril to the diet as a peptogenic before meals leads to more thorough digestion and assimilation and thus saves food.

"The diet may be then cut down from $\frac{1}{4}$ to $\frac{1}{5}$ and the body still be adequately nourished."

Medical Times.

From the review of "Peptogenics in relation to Food Economy," by Dr. J. Campbell, while Food Expert to the Metropolitan Campaign for Food Economy.

The above is but a striking confirmation of what has for years been established to the satisfaction of Scientists and the Medical profession, namely, that the Body-building powers of Bovril are equal from 10 to 20 times the amount of Bovril taken. Take Bovril and save food.

Use Bovril in your cookery, or take it as soup at meals.

136

An interesting little book dealing with the problem of the small household and containing many valuable hints and suggestions for better management with greater comfort. It will be sent free by post to anyone sending a post card application to the British Commercial Gas Association, 47, Victoria Street, Westminster, S.W. 137

138

Because of the shortage of labour on farms the Army Council permitted soldiers to help with agricultural work and harvesting when they could be spared from military duties. 139

139

Within the illustration:
The roughest of the weeds should be cut off & stacked to rot for manure. None of it burned

Stripping turf off trench 3, and putting it into trench 2 to dig into sub-soil as shown here (& in No 1 section)

Soil from No 3 being put into No 2 trench

soil from trench 1 ...cked ready for use for filling the last trench

strips of turf peeled from trench 1 ...cked ready to use for mixing with the ...der-soil of last trench

Soil from No 2 trench

Section showing the sub-soil made by digging (with a fork) the broken up strips of turf into the bottom of the spade-dug trench

1st trench from which soil is taken to other end of plot

140

available land in the cities and suburbs all over the country was dug up and planted with vegetables. Where landowners were reluctant the Government made it clear that it would, if necessary, commandeer the land for others to cultivate. The process was encouraged by the nation's leaders. The King directed that potatoes, cabbages and other vegetables should replace the normal geraniums in the flower-beds surrounding the Queen Victoria Memorial opposite Buckingham Palace and in the royal parks; Lloyd George let it be known that he was growing King Edward potatoes in his garden at Walton Heath; and the Archbishop of Canterbury issued a pastoral letter sanctioning Sunday work. At Alexandra Palace the internees detained there worked substantial allotments to help with their own feeding. By the middle of May an additional half a million acres had been put under cultivation.

Since the Cabinet was against food rationing there was little the Food Controller, Lord Devonport, could do at first except issue exhortations and peripheral regulations about the feeding of game and the sort of food that might be consumed in tea-shops. In February 1917 he issued an appeal

From the national food shortages emerged the allotment system, by which every available plot of land in city and suburb was dug up to grow vegetables. Newspapers and magazines were quick to publish advice on how to set about it.   140

THE ILLUSTRATED LONDON NEWS & SKETCH LTD
EXPRESS DELIVERY
MILFORD LANE, STRAND.

141

On Allotment or Garden.
Rhubarb—the first crop!

Health-giving and delicious with
BIRD'S Nutritious Custard.

Rhubarb is more than usually luscious this mild Spring. It is not only generously rich in its healthful juice, but less acid.

Bird's Custard and Rhubarb both 'feeds' and invigorates. It is spring food of highest health value. In War time, no dish combines so much good food and good health at such small cost.

Bird's
Nutritious Custard

enormously increases the food-value of milk. *Have it to-day with Rhubarb.*

You can laugh at sugar shortage!
BIRD'S Custard made with two good
tablespoonfuls of sugar is sufficient
sweetening for Rhubarb.

C294ᵇ

142

WEBBS' SEEDS

Awarded R.H.S. Gold Medal, Chelsea, 1914.

WEBBS' RE-SELECTED PILOT PEA. (First Early.)
1s. 9d. per pint; 3s. per quart. POST FREE.

All who have Gardens should obtain
WEBBS' GARDEN CATALOGUE.
Beautifully Illustrated. POST FREE.

EDWARD WEBB & SONS (STOURBRIDGE) LTD.,
The King's Seedsmen, STOURBRIDGE.

143

Coal gas as a substitute for petrol was used by some delivery vans, but their range was limited.   141

Rhubarb and custard: another idea for supplementing the wartime rations.   142

Having won a gold medal at Chelsea in 1914, Webbs' reselected pilot pea was no doubt much in demand for allotments.   143

for voluntary rationing, asking citizens to restrict themselves to a weekly maximum of 4lb of bread (or 3lb of flour), 2½lb of meat and ¾lb of sugar. His requested quotas were not adhered to. The poor continued to eat far more than 4lb of bread a week (agricultural labourers were reported to be consuming as much as 14lb) and far less than 2½lb of meat; sugar was often unobtainable. The Food Controller's office was taken to task by Filomena for recommending people to eat the leaves of rhubarb boiled like spinach. Many people had been made exceedingly ill by following this advice, she reported, and urged her readers: 'Don't do it!'

The shortages intensified, and people at home were having to spend more time in queues and in devising other methods of obtaining the supplies they needed. *The Observer* of 8 April 1917 reported: 'The usual weekend potato and coal scenes took place in London yesterday. At Edmonton 131 vehicles were lined up at the gates of a coal depot at nine o'clock in the morning, while the crowd numbered several hundreds. There were also bread and potato queues of such length that the police had to regulate them. In south London trolleymen with coals were besieged by people who had requisitioned all types of receptacles, including perambulators, wheelbarrows, go-carts and trucks, while others brought sacks, baskets and boxes.' Such scenes were becoming commonplace as the country seemed to be facing starvation. At one time it was reported that London had only two days' stock of wheat, with no ships in the Atlantic bringing further supplies. Germany was using its U-boats to wage unrestricted war against all merchant ships sailing to and from allied ports and in April 1917, 542,000 tons of

BETTER FIRES *with* LESS COAL

"Devon" Fires will give you a real means to economy—economy in coal, economy in labour. "Devon" Fires are designed to throw all the heat into the room, and the fuel consumption is small. Further, the fuel is almost completely consumed, only a mere handful of cinders and ash remains. That means economy. Moreover, because the "Devon" Fires are as nearly smokeless as science can make them there is less dirt and dust. That means economy in labour. For better fires and for real economy instal "Devon" Fires—the prices are strictly moderate.

"DEVON" FIRES

Illustrated Price List free from

CANDY & CO., LTD., 87 NEWMAN ST., OXFORD ST., W.
WORKS—HEATHFIELD, NEWTON ABBOT, DEVON.

144

145

Postpone your Holidays.

An appeal to the nation by Sir Douglas Haig.

"Let the whole British Nation forego any idea of a general holiday until our goal is reached. A speedy and decisive victory will then be ours." *Sir Douglas Haig*

This Appeal is addressed not only to Munition Workers, but to all classes of the community.

Support the men at the front.

Postpone your Holidays.

146

An advertisement reflecting the need for economy on fuel and labour.   144

The state not only greatly increased its direct powers over individual freedom during the war, it was also profligate with its advice. On the above poster people were exhorted not to drive motor vehicles for pleasure, not to buy clothes unnecessarily, and not to keep more manservants than they really needed. On the second poster Sir Douglas Haig, the British Commander-in-Chief, appealed to the nation to postpone taking a general holiday until the war was won.   145, 146

British shipping were sunk. Though this proved to be the highest loss in any month of the war, thanks largely to the introduction of the convoy system, substantial tonnages of merchant shipping continued to be sunk and the country remained perilously close to famine. The shortages made themselves felt in many ways. It became an offence to throw rice at weddings; there were restrictions on the use of starch in laundries; the feeding of stray dogs and London pigeons was forbidden; a man was

An experiment in Halifax: a tram-car converted for use as a communal kitchen.   147

Food shortages at home were aggravated by the U-boat attacks on merchant ships crossing the Atlantic. In April 1917 more than 500,000 tons of British shipping were sunk.   148

fined £50 for collecting crusts for pig food; muffins disappeared (and with them the traditional muffin man from the streets of English towns) and bakers were permitted to add potato to their flour, in the proportion of one to seven. Christmas 1917 was the grimmest of the war but for families at home the Ministry of Food suggested a special Christmas dinner made up of ingredients available to all: French rice soup, filleted haddock, roast fowl stuffed with potatoes and chestnuts accompanied by Parisian potatoes and spinach, plum pudding and caramel custard. The cost, for four people, was officially estimated to be 10s, though in fact it was considerably more.

After Christmas the shortages of certain foods became even more apparent. Michael MacDonagh reported on 13 January 1918 that, for the first time in their thirty years of housekeeping, he and his wife were unable to have their weekend joint because the local butcher had none to offer. The following weekend he visited Smithfield to find the retail market thronged with people hoping to get the meat their butchers were unable to provide. He found little meat but a fair supply of alternatives, including fish (herrings at 8d per lb, cod and haddock at 1s 1d), eggs (between 3s and 4s a dozen), tins of boiled beef (3s 4d) and wood pigeons at 2s each. The notice of 'No Rabbits' was up everywhere — the result, he concluded, of profiteering: 'Quite recently rabbits could only be had at the exorbitant price of 4s 9d each. Then the Food Controller stepped in and fixed the price at 2s 9d. Result, the whole supply disappeared, and not a rabbit has been seen in the market since!' The Food Controller had also fixed maximum prices for bread, a 1lb loaf retailing at 2½d and a 4lb one at 9d. These prices involved a

direct state subsidy to millers and bakers amounting to about £45 million a year.

Still there was no rationing. The Food Controller, now Lord Rhondda, argued that it would be difficult to administer and that it would add to the hardships of the poor. To encourage people to reduce their consumption the Food Ministry issued posters advising 'Eat Slowly: You Will Need Less Food', and 'Keep Warm: You Will Need Less Food'. To avoid the problem of queues retailers were required to register their customers. Some grocers would not sell any goods to people who were not registered with them for sugar and sometimes insisted that other purchases were made as well. Mrs Peel noticed an advertisement resulting from such practice: 'Will the lady who overheard salesman refuse to supply a mackerel unless lady bought six pairs of lisle thread stockings or ear trumpet kindly communicate with the Food Controller, Grosvenor House.' Other retailers were accused of sending goods to favoured customers out of the back door while refusing them to people who had queued patiently for an hour or more. These and other abuses such as hoarding led to a growing demand for the introduction of compulsory rationing. By the time rationing was finally introduced, early in 1918, it was greeted with feelings of relief as a welcome, if belated, official recognition of a need which most people had been aware of for a long time. Even when rationing arrived it was introduced with some hesitancy, and in stages.

Local authorities in many parts of the country imposed limited forms of food rationing before the national scheme was introduced. Sugar was generally the first item to be restricted but in February 1918 a general food rationing order was brought into force for London and the Home Counties — Essex, Hertfordshire, Kent, Middlesex, Surrey and Sussex — whose combined population was then about ten million. The items rationed were butcher's meat, bacon, butter, margarine and lard. Each household was issued with two new cards — a 'meat card' for butcher's meat and bacon and a 'food card' for butter, margarine and lard. Sugar cards had already been distributed. The weekly rations were 15oz of beef, mutton, lamb or pork, 5oz of bacon, 4oz of

Compulsory rationing was not introduced until early in 1918. This page from *The Illustrated London News* of 23 February that year (right) showed some of the foods that were rationed and those that were not, and also showed sample pages from the meat cards issued for London and the Home Counties.
149, 150

150

151

152

Pupils in North London, where saving was encouraged by the school authorities, wave their war-saving certificates.   151

An advertisement clearly indicates that not all Britons fully supported the Government's savings campaign.   152

Troops on the streets of Dublin following the Sinn Fein Easter uprising in 1916 — a violent reminder that the Irish question, though dormant for most of the war, remained unresolved.   153

butter, margarine or lard, and 8oz of sugar. It was carefully explained that the basis of the system was fair shares for all and that the rations applied to everyone, including those who lived in Buckingham Palace. The newspaper reported that the King and Queen received their cards from the Westminster food committee and the London and Home Counties meat card issued to Her Majesty the Queen, signed Mary R., was photographed.

In April the rationing scheme was extended to the rest of the country. Queues and complaints virtually disappeared but everyone felt the pinch. Arnold Bennett noted in his *Journal* in 1918 that when people were invited to his house for dinner they were asked to bring some of their own food. Newspapers

and magazines were much preoccupied with food shortages and with recommending new recipes and ideas for using unusual sources of food. In *The Illustrated London News* Filomena extolled the virtues of sorrel, young dandelion leaves and nettles, and passed on to her readers (though with no positive recommendation) a tip from the Japanese Ambassador that the young fronds of the common brake-fern could be boiled (with a good deal of carbonate of soda) to make an acceptable vegetable. G.K. Chesterton, on the other hand, used his column to suggest that there was altogether too much concern with food. He wrote that he was tempted to suggest that the talk about food should also be rationed or at least that 'it should be made clear to our allies, and still more to our enemies, that our population is not in a frenzy about famine because the papers largely consist of warnings and calculations'.

As well as allies and enemies Chesterton might have included 'our men at the front' in his list of those who needed to be reassured about the state of public opinion at home, for he recognised the increasing difference in attitude between the men at the front and those living at home in conditions which inevitably seemed — to those who had experienced the horrors of the trenches — reasonably comfortable and assured. Soldiers returning to

Britain resented the constant carping about such minor irritations as rationing, or the shortage of servants, and the preoccupation with occasional bombing raids which must have seemed insignificant hazards to them. Siegfried Sassoon was one of those soldiers who made public protest, in his 'soldier's declaration' of July 1917 against what he described as the 'political errors and insincerities' for which the fighting men were being sacrificed. He declared that the war of defence and liberation had been transformed into a war of aggression and conquest and was being prolonged by those who had the power to end it. He hoped that his declaration would 'help destroy the callous complacence with which the majority of those at home regard the continuance of agonies which they do not share, and which they have not sufficient imagination to realize''. Edmund Blunden, home on leave from France, was another writer who noted the apparently growing divergence between the men at the front and the civilians at home. He commented on the 'large decay of lively bright love of country, the crystallisation of dull civilian hatred on the basis of "the last drop of blood", and the fact that the German air raids had almost persuaded my London friends that London was the sole battlefront'. There was certainly no doubting the sense of war-weariness that settled over the country after more than three

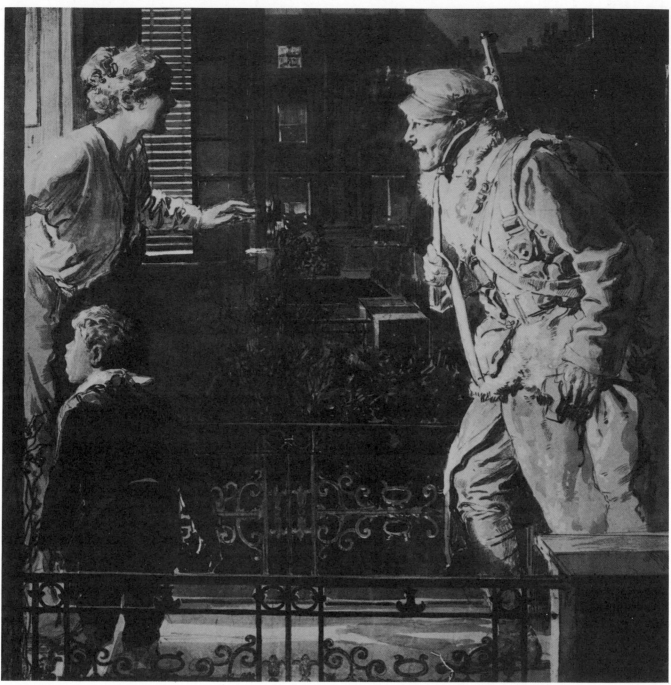

154

years of the struggle. It reflected partly the sheer frustration that, after so long a time and after so many casualties, no progress seemed to have been made on the battle-field; partly the fear that the war could go on for another two years (which was the assumption on which munitions were being manufactured) and partly the growing difficulties of life at home.

One of the most worrying manifestations of this national war-weariness for the Government was an increase in labour unrest. In April and May 1917

Home for Christmas. Two drawings by Matania reflecting the excitement at home when men returned from the trenches for a few days' leave. 154, 155

there were widespread unofficial strikes in Rochdale, Barrow and elsewhere, involving some 200,000 men and the loss of 1,500,000 working days. Lloyd George believed that though agitators were partly responsible they would have been powerless

155

unless there was a basis of genuine discontent. 'The workers were sound at heart,' he wrote, 'but there was a real danger that the hardships, anomalies and annoyances of the times might be worked up by trouble-makers to wear down their sense of patriotic duty.' In June eight area commissions were set up to investigate and report on the causes of discontent. Their reports cited a good number, including high food prices in relation to wages, the unequal distribution of food, the restriction on the mobility of labour, the calling-up of young workers who had been understood to have been immune under the Military Service Acts, lack of adequate housing in some districts, liquor restrictions, industrial fatigue due to Sunday and overtime work, want of confidence in the fulfilment of Government pledges, lack of consideration for women workers by some employers, delays in granting pensions to soldiers, and inadequacy of the compensation payable under the Workmen's Compensation Act. In 1917 for one or more of these reasons, there were 688 'trade disputes' involving 860,000 workers and causing the loss of 5,966,000 working days — higher than in the earlier war years, though fewer than in the years immediately preceding the war. A general increase in wages for all Government work and continuing rigorous control of prices followed the commissions' reports, but diagnosis proved easier than cure. In spite of the German offensive on the Somme launched in March 1918 and the extreme threat it posed to the allies for a few desperate months, industrial disputes continued to hamper the war effort at home. Engineers went on strike in Birmingham and Leeds, munition workers downed tools in protest against further dilution, miners protested against the emergency recruitment of young men from the pits (but withdrew their objections when Lloyd George summoned their leaders to Downing Street and showed them a map of the situation at the front) and even the London police went on strike in support of their demands for higher pay and union recognition. For three days the metropolitan area, which stretched from Barnet to Epsom, was without its blue-uniformed 'bobbies'. The Guards and the 'Specials' took over, and law and order prevailed.

6 LEISURE AND PLEASURE

As the burdens and tragedies of war grew heavier the need for some refuge from the daily hardships and annoyances became stronger. Moreover, under the influence of war, people's attitudes towards what was permissible in social behaviour changed and so new forms of leisure activities developed. With more people in jobs and working longer hours, there was certainly less time available for leisure; but most people had more money to spend. With the added stimulus of brief appearances of soldiers on leave there was a general determination to balance hard work with concentrated enjoyment. This was particularly conspicuous among the young, who were less content to spend their evenings at home than they had been before the war, and also among women who had acquired a new independence as a result of the opportunities of war work. This took many of them away from home and into hostels and lodgings. As the casualty lists grew so did the determination to have a good time while the opportunity still existed. The desire to forget the horrors of war for a few hours led to an increase in many of the pleasures that were officially disapproved of, including drinking, smoking, drug-taking, dancing, gambling and sex.

The increase in drinking led to the Government action described in Chapter 3, but there was also increasing concern at what was seen as a rising tide of 'immorality', by which was generally meant a more relaxed view of sex compared with the attitudes that had prevailed before the war. The Army recognised the dangers and gave every new recruit, along with his pay-book, a note bearing advice from Lord Kitchener to avoid any intimacy with women. This advice was not made any easier to follow by the presence of many reputable women round the training camps and in the towns where soldiers spent their leave — a presence explained in the following terms by Mrs Helena Swanwick: 'If millions of men were to be killed in early manhood, or even boyhood, it behoved every young women to secure a mate and replenish the population while there was yet time.' Another woman historian of the time, M.A. Hamilton, put it this way: 'Life was less than cheap; it was thrown away. The religious teaching that the body was the temple of the Holy Ghost could mean little or nothing to those who saw it mutilated and destroyed in millions by Christian nations engaged in war. All moral standards were held for a short moment and irretrievably lost. Little wonder that the old ideals of chastity and self-control in sex were, for many, also lost.' Statistically the result was that between 1914 and 1918 the rate of

DUBARRY'S BATH SALTS

These Bath Salts give the bath water a rain-like softness, are tonic, invigorating, refreshing, and beautifying in their effect on the skin.

They are supplied in eighteen Exquisite Odours, the principal of which are :

"THE HEART OF A ROSE"	**"ELDORADO"**
"ARCADIE"	**"EAU DE COLOGNE"**
"ROMADOR"	**"NUIT DE MAI"**
"BLUE LAGOON"	**"A BUNCH OF VIOLETS"**
"NIGHT OF JUNE"	**"APRÈS LA PLUIE"**
"RAVANA"	**"GARDEN OF KAMA"**

IN BOXES AT

2/6   4/6   8/6   17/6   and   42/-   each.

BATH DUSTING POWDER

In same sizes and prices as Bath Salts.   For use with a large puff after the bath.

Sent post free on receipt of remittance.

157

The hard grind of war was relieved by short periods of concentrated enjoyment, much of it centred on London's West End where, as in this café scene, the British would be joined by their off-duty allies in arms.   156

The new freedom that women gained from the war reflected in their manners and customs. They smoked cigarettes and began freely to use cosmetics.   157, 158

illegitimacy increased by thirty per cent. There were also dramatic increases in the number of marriages, particularly early marriages, and in the divorce rate.

The moral freedom that women displayed was reflected in their manners and fashions. Before 1914 young ladies who valued their reputation could not walk alone in the streets of London; a London magistrate had even pronounced that a woman doing so after ten o'clock at night must expect to be molested. The war rapidly changed such assumptions. Women went unescorted into restaurants,

158

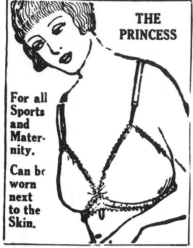

frequented public houses, smoked cigarettes in public places, began freely to use cosmetics and adopted the brassière in place of the traditional camisole. Almost as soon as the war began skirts were raised above the ankles and then lifted again to about mid-calf. There was considerable opposition, notably from the Northcliffe newspapers, but the obvious advantages of the short skirt for women working in factories and on buses and trains, and the requirements of the women's forces, ensured its survival against such disapproval before long trousers, worn by women working on the land, also became acceptable even when worn off duty, though Mrs Peel noted some continuing opposition to the style: 'So comfortable did women find their two-legged dress that some land girls preferred to wear their breeches when off duty and were reported to their superior officers for so doing. These ladies refused to interfere, their opinion being that the dress was a decent and honourable uniform which

the public should respect as it respected the uniform of the soldier. In munition works there was at first some difficulty about trousers, for the women were very sensitive to any ridicule from the men. It took some time to popularise them, chiefly because the men laughed about them and also because some of the older women thought them indecent.'

The relative prosperity of the war years enabled more people to eat out and to go to dance-halls and night-clubs which gained new popularity with the spread of ragtime and jazz and the dance music of American composers such as Jerome Kern and Irving Berlin. Although night-clubs were ordered, in 1915, to close at 10.30 p.m. — a regulation popularly known as the 'beauty sleep order' — the effect was simply to drive the clubs and their patrons underground. The demand for the clubs was such that as soon as one was closed another took its place. The Soho area of London became the focal point of these clubs and by the end of 1915 it was

160

estimated that there were 150 of them in this area alone. Soho also thrived as a centre of restaurants and as a shopping area both for food and for clothing, particularly for the ready-made dresses much in demand by working women for their off-duty hours.

The theatre had been a great preoccupation of the Edwardians but, though the theatres remained popular throughout the war, there was little development in terms of serious drama. Few memorable new plays were put on and even Bernard Shaw found the war uncongenial to creative effort; he produced nothing for the theatre between *Pygmalion* in 1913 and *Heartbreak House* in 1919.

The new freedom for women was also reflected in their clothes. They adopted the brassière in place of the traditional camisole, and dressed more casually to go unescorted into restaurants and other public places. 159, 160, 161

162

163

164

165

Skirts were raised above the ankles almost as soon as war began and were soon lifted to mid-calf. The blouse was advertised as being thoroughly practical for women workers.   162, 163

A lounge suit from Harrods, 1918 style.   164

A 'note of originality' from Burberrys.   165

Tea-pyjamas, described when they appeared in 1918 as being 'the latest attack on the skirt'.   166

Among the dances that came and went with bewildering rapidity was 'The Pigeon Walk', here danced by George Grossmith and Peggy Kurton in the musical *Tonight's the Night* at The Gaiety Theatre.   167

Although Shakespeare at the Old Vic always commanded full houses the demand was generally for lighter fare. Most popular of all, at least in terms of its length of run, was *Chu Chin Chow*, a sort of sophisticated pantomime, which ran for more than 2,000 performances. Another favourite was *The Bing Boys Are Here*, in which George Robey and Violet Loraine sang 'If You Were the Only Girl in the World'. Musical revues with scantily-dressed chorus-girls were also greatly in popular demand in spite of the opposition they aroused among some representatives of the older generations and the wrath of some poets like Siegfried Sassoon:

> The House is crammed: tier beyond tier they grin
> And cackle at the Show, while prancing ranks
> of harlots shrill the chorus, drunk with din;
> 'We're sure the Kaiser loves our dear old Tanks!'
> I'd like to see a Tank come down the stalls,
> Lurching to rag-time tunes, or 'Home, sweet Home,'
> And there'd be no more jokes in music-halls
> To mock the riddled corpses round Bapaume.

Audiences in general did not share sentiments of

169

Most popular of the wartime shows was *Chu Chin Chow*, which ran for more than 2,000 performances at His Majesty's Theatre. 168

A scene from *The Bing Boys are Here*, which starred George Robey. 169

The composers of 'It's a Long Way to Tipperary', Mr Harry Williams and Mr Jack Judge (left and right), with their publisher, Mr Bert Feldman (centre). 170

this nature. They wanted to be entertained and were ready to guffaw at jokes against the 'Hun', and to cheer at patriotic references to British 'Tommies'. The National Anthem was played at the close of all performances in the theatre and in the cinema, a custom initiated in the First World War which survived until well after the Second.

For a growing number of people the cinema became a primary source of entertainment during

170

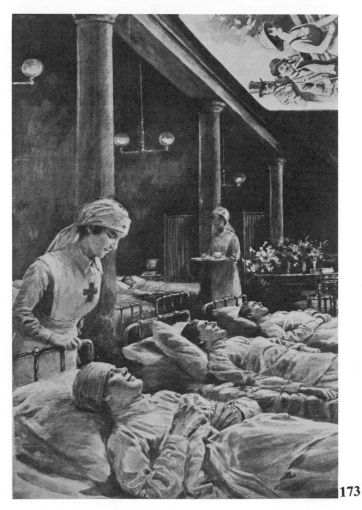

Mr Will Evans, the revue artist, photographed in his car with his children alongside.   171

Advertisement for the Aeolian gramophone, produced in 1917.   172

Films projected on a hospital ceiling for bedridden wounded soldiers at a hospital in France.   173

The cinema created a vast new audience during the war, helped by stars such as Charlie Chaplin and Mary Pickford, here photographed on the shoulders of Douglas Fairbanks.   174

174

175

Lady Diana Manners, photographed after she had taken a course of training in nursing at Guy's Hospital and was about, as *The Sketch* magazine described it, to desert the drawing-room for the wards. 175

the First World War. There were about 3,000 cinemas in Britain in 1914 and these rapidly grew in number during the next four years. The National Council of Public Morals published a study in 1917 which noted that films — these were, of course, all silent — had created a new audience, the vast majority of cinema-goers not usually attending any other places of amusement, and most of them occupying the cheaper seats. The Council could not altogether approve of the cinema's growing popularity, fearing the effect on public morals of a form of entertainment which had to take place in the dark. A Board of Censors had been established in 1912 to issue certificates — 'U' for universal, meaning films regarded as suitable for everyone to see, including children, and 'A' for those suitable only for an adult audience. In addition cinemas had supervisors to ensure that audiences did not indulge in any indecent behaviour when the lights went down. These supervisors soon disappeared, presumably called to more vital war service, but the Council of Public Morals maintained its concern that adequate supervision should be exercised and campaigned for a stricter censorship of unwholesome and suggestive films. It did not accept the arguments of the film-makers and exhibitors that they could only provide profitably what the public would watch. The films which the public actually saw were made in America, the vast majority of them purely escapist in character, though D.W. Griffith's *Birth of a Nation* and *Intolerance* and the comedies of Charlie Chaplin made in Hollywood during the war were already demonstrating that the film could claim to be a new art form.

In its arguments with the makers and distributors of films the National Council of Public Morals suggested that they were inclined to rate both the intelligence and the conscience of the public rather lower than they actually were. The Government was certainly guilty of making this mistake when, in 1916, it decided to close the London art galleries and museums 'for reasons of economy'. Though most people did not visit such institutions regularly and attendances declined in the first year of the war, this decision provoked such an outcry that it was quickly reversed. In the later years of the war attendances rapidly increased, particularly at the National Gallery. One of the more social annual events of the art world, the Royal Academy Private View, was seen to have lost something of its pre-war glory, as Filomena reported on the 'Ladies' Page' of *The Illustrated London News* in May 1918:

'At the threshold one missed the bank of flowers

that always adorned either side of the wide staircase; and within the rooms there was no crowd — certainly not one-third of the number of visitors there used invariably to be. Moreover those who were present were garbed with a more commonplace plainness and quietness that contrasted strongly with the show of happier days, when this was the first of the great society gatherings of the season, and therefore the occasion for the earliest display of spring fashions. This year, not one solitary costume was in any way strikingly original, handsome, or in any way remarkable. Where is there a person who is not suffering family and friendly and financial losses that make display and frivolity seem folly? As I entered, I met a Countess in a black-and-white pin-stripe coat-frock, and a black toque of Tagel straw with a jet plaque for sole trimming. In the hall I saw another Peeress — one of the richest women in England, but a bereaved mother — wearing an old-fashioned black satin dress made with a train to lie a few inches on the ground, and a hat with a plain stretched white satin crown and an outstanding upturned brim of black tulle. True it is that both these Peeresses, as well as many other women there, had added handsome pearl necklaces and fur stoles to these ultra-plain gowns, but these adornments were undoubtedly pre-war possessions. Throughout the rooms the tale was the same. It is worthwhile to say this, that the working classes may not be deceived and irritated by the false supposition that ''Society'' is going on as usual, indifferent to the nation's losses.'

And what of the paintings at the 1918 Summer Exhibition? Filomena did not rate them very highly. She reported that there were a great many pictures by women on the walls but nothing particularly striking. There were, however, quite a number of canvases depicting women at their novel wartime occupations in factory and field, and Filomena's eye was also caught by a portrait of Miss Iris Van Raalte 'in a blue velvet cap and blue velvet and biscuit canvas striped cloak, who is painted with a half-smoked cigarette between her fingers'.

The strains of war seemed also to increase the demand for good music. This was readily available largely through the efforts of Sir Thomas Beecham, for although opera at Covent Garden was abandoned during the war and the opera house was used by the Government to store furniture Beecham's English Opera group played throughout the war both in London and the provinces. In his auto-biography, *A Mingled Chime*, he gave his own explanation of its success, which he attributed to a combination of a high mood of idealism in the

176

A painting from the 1918 Royal Academy exhibition: *Their Majesties King George V and Queen Mary Visiting the Battle Districts of France*, by Frank O. Salisbury. **176**

public, and economic stringency in the musical profession. 'In wartime,' he wrote, 'the temper of a section of the people for a while becomes graver, simpler, and more concentrated. The opportunities for recreation and amusement are more restricted, transport is limited, and the thoughtful intelligence craves and seeks these antidotes to a troubled conscience of which great music is perhaps the most potent.' As conductor of the Hallé Orchestra, Beecham took advantage of the nation's patriotic mood to introduce much unfamiliar English music to his audiences but he did not abandon the classical repertoire and was able to restore German music after a short, patriotic interval at the beginning of

177

composers, but a notice in the programme indicated that Sir Henry Wood had no intention of allowing this to continue. The Wagner programme was given on the following Monday and for the rest of the war there was no boycott of German music at the Proms.

Among the most popular entertainments sport, and those who watched it, probably suffered the most severely during the war years. Professional football was abandoned for the duration in the spring of 1915 and cricket, racing and the university boat race were also stopped. This deprived many ordinary men of their most enjoyable entertainment, leaving them with the consolations of the reduced hours in the pubs, the occasional outing and the fireside pleasure of reading. Outings were infrequent (because of the limitations on transport and other reasons) but some traditional celebrations were maintained. One was the fair on Hampstead Heath which was visited by Michael MacDonagh on the third Whit Monday of the war. He found its vitality as remarkable as ever but noted also some significant changes:

'The crowd was not so large, and was less varied in its elements. More children than adults, more females than males, were to be seen, and of the latter

the war. Sir Henry Wood's promenade concerts at the Queen's Hall, begun in 1895, were also continued throughout the war with increasing popular support. There was trouble at the start of the first season, in August 1914, when the traditional Monday night Wagner concert had to be replaced by a programme of British, French and Russian

178

Though Covent Garden was used as a furniture store throughout the war Sir Thomas Beecham kept the English Opera Group playing both in London and the provinces. The scene from the third act of *La Bohème* was from the 1917 Aldwych production with Bessie Tyas as Mimi and Maurice D'Oisly as Rudolph. 177

Though regular horse racing was abandoned for the duration occasional substitutes were held. The Racecourse Association Steeplechase in March 1916, run at Gatwick, took the place of the Grand National. 178

Ten shillings would buy a camera, and the separations enforced by war greatly increased the interest in and importance of home photography. 179

In addition to the normal weekly issue *The Illustrated London News* also published throughout the war a weekly pictorial record of the war. 180

Because of the wartime limitations on transport, holiday entertainments were generally home-made and local, as was this Red Cross pageant at Esher Place on Whit Monday, 1918. 181

179

180

the comparatively few that were of military age, when accosted by the Assistant Provost-Marshals who roamed the Heath, produced papers which afforded reasons of one kind or another why they were not in Khaki. The usual boisterousness was also much abated .... The Food Controller would have seen in the eating-booths no breach of his regulations. Gone were the piles of pork-pies and pigs' trotters that before the war used to make a gargantuan feast of the holiday at Whitsuntide; gone, too, were the heaps of the round parti-coloured sugarstick known as rock, and the thick bars of chocolate. Very little wheaten bread was on sale. What was commonly served with the cup of tea was a chunk of treacly brown cake.'

For his reading matter the stay-at-home might have book, magazine or newspaper. The popular Press was, by now, well established but it suffered from the restrictions imposed by wartime censorship. There was less restraint on pictures, which provided an opportunity for publications specialising in pictorial reporting. *The Illustrated London News* published throughout the war not only its usual weekly issue, which appeared every Friday, but also an additional weekly pictorial history, appearing each Wednesday, called *The Illustrated War News*. The most popular books, like the films and the theatre, were lightweight, mainly novels by writers such as Nat Gould, Victoria Cross and Edgar Wallace although there were also authors of greater literary quality, including Arnold Bennett, G.K. Chesterton, H.G. Wells, James Joyce, D.H. Lawrence, Aldous Huxley, Lytton Strachey, Bernard Shaw, Somerset Maugham,

181

Thomas Hardy and Rudyard Kipling. None of them produced their greater works during the war, which proved to be a more productive time for the poets. T.S. Eliot's first volume of verse, *Prufrock and other Observations*, was published in 1917 and the war generated its own poets — Rupert Brooke, Robert Graves, Isaac Rosenburg, Edmund Blunden, Wilfred Owen — who accurately mirrored the prevailing attitudes of these years: the heroic, patriotic fervour of the first months, the disillusion and despair of the later years.

The war generated its own poets, who accurately reflected the prevailing attitudes of the times. The first heroic, patriotic fervour was elegantly expressed by Rupert Brooke, who died in 1915 when on his way to the Dardanelles.   182

War games as played by one of the leading writers of the day, Mr H.G. Wells. Early in the war Wells wrote to *The Times* urging the British public to organise itself against invasion. 'If we find German soldiers in England one morning,' he wrote, 'we are going to fight.'   183

182

183

The disillusion and despair of the later years of war was recorded in the poems of Wilfred Owen, who was killed in action in November 1918. His photograph was included in the roll of honour pages (third row, extreme right) which were a regular feature of the illustrated magazines throughout the war.   184

THE ROLL OF HONOUR

THE FOLLOWING OFFICERS HAVE ALL DIED IN THE SERVICE
OF THEIR COUNTRY, EITHER IN ACTION, FROM WOUNDS, OR
OTHER CAUSES DIRECTLY INCIDENTAL TO THE GREAT WAR

Capt. N. M. North, M.C.
Northumberland Fusiliers.
He was the only son of Mr.
Harry North of South Africa

Captain C. Martineau
Royal Warwickshire Regt.
He was the eldest son of
Mr. G. A. Martineau

Capt. A. Vernon Jones
Royal Welsh Fusiliers. He
enlisted in September, 1914.
Son of Mr. R. Jones

Captain P. Hewetson
Loyal North Lancs. Regt.
Gazetted in August, 1914.
He was educated at Repton

Capt. S. F. Terry, M.C.
Wilts. Regt. Now presumed
killed last March near Ba-
paume. Son of Mr. T. Terry

Lieut. F. G. B. Thomas
Essex Regt. He was the only son of
Major and Mrs. N. Thomas. Presumed
killed at Krithia, Gallipoli, in 1915

**Lieutenant
E. F. Lowther**
Trench Mortar Battery. He
enlisted in 1914 and was
gazetted early in 1917. He
fell in action last June

**Lieutenant
G. W. Board**
E. Surrey Rgt. (attd. R.F.C.)
He was missing since
November 30, 1917, and is
now presumed killed

**Lieutenant
E. J. W. Whitehead**
R.G.A. He rejoined the
Artists' Rifles in January,
1915, and was given a com-
mission in November, 1916

**2nd Lieut. H. D. Etheridge,
M.M., M.C.**
Royal Fusiliers. He won the Military
Medal in June, 1917, and a bar to it
a month later. Killed in action

2nd Lieut. M. F. Oliphant
Norfolk Regiment. He was educated
at Rugby and Pembroke College,
Oxford, and was the son of the
Rev. F. G. Oliphant

**Paymaster Lieutenant
Louis Needham, D.S.C.**
Royal Naval Reserve. He
was the second son of Mr.
and Mrs. J. B. Needham

**2nd Lieutenant
H. E. Randall**
King's Shropshire L.I.
Died of wounds. Son of
Mr. and Mrs. G. E. Randall

**Captain N. E. E.
Burton Fanning**
R.M.L.I. Educated at Rep-
ton. Son of Dr. and Mrs.
Burton Fanning of Norwich

2nd Lieut. W. E. S. Owen, M.C.
Manchester Regt. He was the eldest
son of Mr. and Mrs. T. Owen, and
was killed in action near the Sambre
Canal on November 4, 1918

Lieut.-Col. W. S. M. Palmer
Northumberland Fusiliers. He was
given a commission in September,
1914, and went to the front in November of the same year

**Captain
H. R. Gladstone**
Northumberland Fusiliers.
He was the son of Mr.
Gladstone of Consett, Dur-
ham, and was educated at
Durham School. Killed in
1918 while leading his men
near Beaumont Hamel

**Captain
H. F. Mott, M.C.**
London Regt. He was
educated at Marlborough
and Oxford. Eldest son of
Mr. A. F. Mott

**Lieutenant
A. B. Mott**
R.N., H.M.S. "Conqueror."
He was the second son of
Mr. and Mrs. A. F. Mott,
and entered the Royal
Naval College, Dartmouth,
in Sept., 1911. Appointed to
the "Conqueror" in 1916

Lieut.-Col. W. R. Brakspear
Indian Infantry. He was gazetted
in 1887 and transferred to the Indian
Army two years later. He went to
the front in 1914

Pro Patria mori

184

7 A COUNTRY FIT FOR HEROES?

The manifestations of discontent and war-weariness that began to be so evident at home in 1917 did not sap the general determination that the struggle against Germany had to go on. Talk of peace negotiations was not popularly acceptable. The Government no doubt accurately reflected this mood when it rejected attempts at negotiation by the American President, Woodrow Wilson. It took its cue partly from the lack of public support for the demands for negotiation put up by individual pacifists and also by the Union of Democratic Control, whose meetings were sometimes broken up by soldiers on leave and whose secretary, E.D. Morel, was imprisoned. G.K. Chesterton argued, in *The Illustrated London News*, that it would be wicked as well as senseless to make peace with Prussia because the result of a peace effected by compromise would simply be the spread of Prussianism. 'All our blows against it would not only be wasted, they would count as blows on the Prussian side. They would glorify not our sword, but his shield. The superstition that the soldier of North Germany is unconquerable and therefore (by his own philosophy) infallible, would be much more firmly established than if there had never been a war at all.' In November 1917 the publication, in *The Daily Telegraph*, of a letter from Lord Lansdowne advocating peace by negotiation (a proposal he had circulated to the Cabinet a year earlier), aroused a storm of protest and confirmed the general view, if confirmation was needed, that the continuing 'hardships, anomalies and annoyances' could only be ultimately justified if victory was total. The Archbishop of Canterbury echoed the mood of the majority when he spoke in Westminster Abbey on a national day of prayer early in 1918. 'We persist,' he said, 'and we must persist in our task' — a civilian precursor of General Haig's celebrated battle order issued in April 1918: 'There is no other course open to us but to fight it out! Every position must be held to the last man; there must be no retirement. With our backs to the wall and believing in the justice of our cause, each one of us must fight to the end.'

Concentration on winning the war did not altogether prevent men from looking ahead to what had to be done, or what they wanted to be done, once it was over. Lloyd George had formulated Britain's war aims — obtaining the agreement of the Cabinet and the Dominions before making them

185

A National Day of Prayer was called for the first Sunday in January 1918, when a proclamation from the King was read in churches throughout the land. In it the King declared that victory would only be gained if we 'ask the blessing of Almighty God upon our endeavour'. The illustration shows the proclamation being read at Westminster Abbey. 185

The King decorated Private T. Hughes with the Victoria Cross at an investiture in Hyde Park. Though wounded during an engagement on the western front, Private Hughes remained in the firing line and then proceeded to capture an enemy machine-gun single-handed. 186

Evening Play Centres for children, first set up at the turn of the century, became more popular during the war, when there were thirty-two centres in London and many more elsewhere. The founder, Mrs Humphrey Ward, noted in her report in the last year of the war that many of the children attending the centres 'were the sons and daughters of men who died for England'. 187

Described as 'ideal housing conditions', these buildings were designed as a 'garden village' to house workers employed by a company at Hendon aerodrome. 188

186

187

188

public, in typically unconventional manner — in an address to a Labour conference held at the Caxton Hall in London on 5 January 1918. He said that Britain's objects in the war were to defend the violated public law of Europe, to vindicate treaty obligations and to secure the restoration of Belgium. 'We are fighting for a just and lasting peace — and we believe that before permanent peace can be hoped for three conditions must be fulfilled. First, the sanctity of treaties must be re-established; secondly a territorial settlement must be secured based on the right of self-determination or the consent of the governed; and lastly, we must seek by the creation of some international organisation to limit the burden of armaments and diminish the probability of war.' Early in 1918 a committee under the chairmanship of Sir Walter (later Lord) Phillimore was appointed to examine the proposal for a 'League of Nations', an idea which originated in discussions in the Fabian Society early in the war, and his report formed the basis of the international organisation which was set up at the peace conference after the war.

At home the determination to look ahead and plan for better things to come was demonstrated by the creation in 1918 of a Ministry of Reconstruction. Though it was not significant for its achievements the Ministry was important as a symbol of the national interest in social reform, also indicated by the passing of the Representation of the People Act (referred to in Chapter 4 above), and the Education Act, both of which won the approval of Parliament

shortly before the end of the war. The Education Act was the work of H.A.L. Fisher, a university professor who had been given political responsibility for education when he was appointed President of the Board of Education by Lloyd George in 1916. The Act provided for entirely free elementary education up to the age of fourteen (the minimum school-leaving age had previously been twelve though during the war some exceptions were made

189

troops in France at about the same time. The epidemic spread through Britain in three waves, the first in mid-July, the second in the first week of November and the third in February 1919. Altogether it was estimated that nearly three-quarters of the population were affected and a total of 151,446 were killed, the vast majority being civilians.

The end of the war came almost as abruptly as it had begun. Turkey surrendered on 30 October and Austria-Hungary on 3 November. The Kaiser fled from Germany and abdicated on 9 November and on 11 November the armistice was signed. In London the conclusion of war was proclaimed by boy scouts on bicycles blowing their bugles (which had been the way of sounding the 'all clear' after air raids) and by the firing of maroons, which was the warning that a raid was about to take place. Michael MacDonagh recalled the suddenness with which peace actually arrived:

'This morning at eleven o'clock I was startled by the booming of maroons, fired from police and fire-brigade stations, the loud reports of those near at

as an emergency measure), and for further part-time education to the age of eighteen. Arrangements were also made for the extension of higher education, for physical training in schools, and for the establishment of nursery schools for children under school age. Though many of these proposals did not survive the economy campaigns of later years (they proved to be much more expensive than Fisher had estimated), they were a clear indication of the resolution that then existed to create, out of the social and economic conditions imposed by the war, a nation better than before the war started — to make Britain, in Lloyd George's graphic phrase, 'a fit country for heroes to live in'.

On the eve of the war's end the country was hit by the epidemic of influenza, commonly known as the 'Spanish 'flu', which started in the Near East and spread across Europe in late summer — though an earlier outbreak of the disease had occurred in the Navy at Scapa Flow in the spring and among the

191

hand being faintly re-echoed by others afar off. As it is six months since these warnings of an air raid have been heard in London (our last bombardment by the enemy having occurred in May), I wondered what they could now imply, so early in the morning. Looking through my window I saw passers by stopping each other and exchanging remarks before hurrying on. They were obviously excited but unperturbed. I rushed out and inquired what was the matter. ''The Armistice,'' they exclaimed. ''The War is over!''

'I was stunned by the news, as if something highly improbable and difficult of belief had happened. It is not that what the papers had been saying about an Armistice had passed out of my mind, but that I had not expected the announcement of its success would have come so soon, and, above all, be proclaimed with the ill-omened maroons. Yet it was so. What is still more curious is that when I became fully seized of the tremendous nature of the event, though I was emotionally disturbed, I felt no joyous exultation. There was relief that the War was over, because it could not now end, as it might have done, in the crowning tragedy of the defeat of the Allies. I

sorrowed for the millions of young men who had lost their lives; and perhaps more so for the living than the dead — for the bereaved mothers and wives whose reawakened grief must in this hour of triumph be unbearably poignant. But what gave me the greatest shock was my feeling in regard to myself. A melancholy took possession of me when I came to realise, as I did quickly and keenly, that a great and unique episode in my life was past and gone, and, as I hoped as well as believed, would never be repeated. Our sense of the value of life and its excitements, so vividly heightened by the War, is, with one final leap of its flame today, about to expire in its ashes. Tomorrow we return to the monotonous and the humdrum. ''So sad, so strange, the days that are no more!'''

London, MacDonagh reported, lost control of itself. Schools, shops, offices and other places of work hurriedly closed, and everyone poured into the streets. MacDonagh himself went to the Houses of Parliament noticing, on the way, a newspaper bill (the first for years because they had been prohibited in order to save paper) proclaiming 'Fighting has ceased on all fronts', and he was in time to hear, at

On 19 July 1919, more formal victory parades and celebrations took place, with dancing through the night at many London hotels.   192

An advertisement from *The Sphere* of November 1918. P.G. Wodehouse's novel *Piccadilly Jim* was published in that year and may perhaps have inspired the advertisement's caption-writer.   193

A U-boat anchored in St Katharine's Dock in the Thames — one of four brought up river after the German surrender.   194

192

GERTIE : " How absolutely topping of you, Bertie, thinking of Chocs ; and I've got ' Army Clubs ' for you."

BERTIE : " Good egg—sweets for the sweet and ' Army Clubs ' for the Army. Birds of a feather sort of flocking together. What !"

"CAVANDERS'

ARMY CLUB "

CIGARETTES.

193

noon, the first striking of Big Ben since the beginning of the war. Thereafter he followed the crowds to Buckingham Palace, where the cry 'We Want King George' brought the King and Queen repeatedly to the balcony, the Queen waving a tiny Union Jack above her head. Mrs Peel recounted the impressions of a young girl who was working in the War Office, and who joined the crowds outside the Palace, as she had four years earlier when war had been declared:

'I thought of the night we were at the Palace at the beginning of the war .... It was a very different sight from that of that August night, with its deep blue sky and the beds of scarlet geraniums and brightly lighted streets and houses. Now it was a grey November morning, the roads were muddy, the lake in St James's Park drained and full of huts. Practically all the men were now in khaki. As in August, the crowd was composed of all sorts and kinds of people — but we should have rubbed our eyes in 1914 if we had seen some of those who mingled in the 1918 crowd — munition girls in bright overalls, who arrived in large lorries, shouting and beating tin tea-trays and waving flags, staff

194

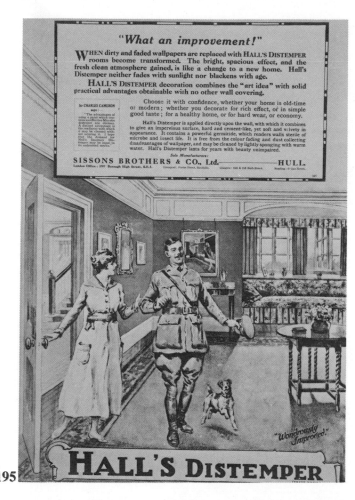

officers in cars driven by smart khaki girls, and cars from the Admiralty with their even smarter "Wren" chauffeuses, and everywhere men in hospital blue. The people in the Palace were getting a balcony all decked out ready for the King to appear: men with mops scrambled up on ladders and swept the walls, taking a quite unnecessarily long time to do it; then came housemaids who were so pleased with their reception by the crowd that they dawdled about to take the cheers.'

It was clear enough to those who shouted for the King outside Buckingham Palace or stood in the streets to greet him as he drove for five successive days through the poorer parts of London that

Cleaning up. An advertisement of the time shows an officer returning to his home from the war to find it newly-distempered, and repairs to Oxford Street in 1919 following the neglect of war years.   195, 196

A party of New Zealand soldiers with the English brides they married during their stay preparing to return home at the end of the war.   197

The National Debt rose by £7,000 million during the war, and servicing it took nearly half the yield from taxation. To succeed the War Loan, the Government floated another when war ended, called the Victory Loan.   198

PROSPERITY

Ensure future
prosperity by
making

Victory Loan

a gigantic
Success.

Britain could never be quite the same after the experience of the First World War, though the fundamental social structure of the nation was less radically altered than might have been expected by such a convulsion. The most obvious immediate consequence was the loss of life. About 760,000 Britons had been killed, of whom some 614,000 were servicemen, 145,000 merchant seamen and 1,117 were civilians. They represented nearly ten per cent of all men under forty-five years of age, which not only altered the population balance but also caused the emotional and other, less easily defined, damage associated with the loss of men described as the cream of their generation — many of whom had been the first to volunteer and who formed the young officers in the front line. A second powerful social effect of the war was its cost. The National Debt rose by £7,000 million and wholesale prices by the end of the war were 140 per cent above those in 1914, representing a decline in the value of the pound to the equivalent of 8s 3d in pre-war money. The physical damage suffered was estimated by J.M. Keynes in 1919 at £570 million, but subsequent estimates put the figure at least twice as high. The immediate economic consequences were high taxation and increasing inflation. There was also a severe housing shortage. Various forms of rationing continued, the last of which, on sugar, was not ended until November 1920. Industrial unrest again

199

became persistent — in 1919 there were an average of 100,000 workers on strike on each day of the year.

The war created expectations but at the same time reduced the nation's opportunities of meeting them. Nonetheless some social changes quickly became apparent. The number of taxpayers had increased by more than six times. The landed classes ceased to occupy their former position of social and political primacy, the balance having moved from the landed to the business interest. The upper classes also found it difficult to return to the lavish standards of Edwardian days — though some of the traditional pleasures of the wealthy, including the London season and fox-hunting, were quickly restored.

The severe housing shortage after the war was illustrated by the artist, Bryan de Grineau, and showed conditions inside a house in Shoreditch, in the East End of London, where four adults and seven children shared one room in which they had to eat, sleep and live. 199

The London season returned in 1919, and with it Royal Ascot. 200

A railway strike in the autumn of 1919 caused problems for London commuters, here shown scrambling to get on a tram on the Thames Embankment. 201

200

201

The traditional Sunday morning display of the fashionable in Hyde Park.   202

The Coalition Cabinet formed by Lloyd George in November 1919.   203

Clemenceau, the French Premier, addresses the German delegates at the Trianon Palace Hotel, Versailles, on 7 May 1919. 'The time has come when we must settle our accounts,' he said, presenting the Germans with the Allied conditions for the peace treaty.   204

The victory parade passes through Trafalgar Square and under Admiralty Arch on 19 July 1919.   205

206

207

Summer holiday 1919: the beach at Eastbourne.
206

The post-war boom in Britain was short-lived and many of the returning soldiers were disillusioned by what they found at home. Some opted for opportunities overseas, such as that offered by South Africa in this advertisement. **207**

Returning soldiers, many of whom had gone straight from school to military service, found themselves without any qualifications for pursuing a career and had to resume their studies. The photograph shows officers in a laboratory at Cambridge University in 1919. **208**

The cenotaph in Whitehall, unveiled by the King on 11 November 1920. 209

Inequality in the division of wealth remained very pronounced, for in the 1920s two-thirds of the nation's wealth was owned by less than three per cent of the population. The salaried class showed a substantial increase during the war years — from around 1,500,000 before the war to more than 2,700,000 in 1921, when they formed twenty-two per cent of the working population. The growth occurred mainly among the professional classes, civil servants, the managerial class and among women. At the lower end of the social scale the working class also emerged from the war with some advantages. Wage rates had been doubled, the average working week reduced from fifty-five hours to forty-eight, and organised labour, as a result of the wartime need for maximising production, had been greatly strengthened. On the political side the Labour Party continued to grow and was given additional significance after the 'coupon' election — so-called because favoured candidates of the Coalition received the endorsement of Lloyd George, now hailed as the man who won the war. The election, hastily held in 1918 at Lloyd George's insistence, returned only fifty-seven Labour MPs compared with 474 for the Coalition, but as the Labour Party had formally withdrawn from the Coalition it became the official Opposition party, which enabled it to benefit from the disintegration of Lloyd George's Government in the early 1920s.

The years immediately after the war were boom years, which enabled four million demobilised men to be absorbed quickly into industry. But the boom was short-lived, and many of the returning soldiers were soon disillusioned by what they found at home. After the battle for survival there seemed little enthusiasm for a struggle of a different kind, and one more difficult to portray in the black-and-white terms of total war — that of overcoming the nation's economic difficulties. In spite of the changes, the brave new world that had been expected to emerge from the war seemed, to many, to be disappointingly like the old.

208

209

SELECTED BIBLIOGRAPHY

Annual Register, The, 1914-20

W. Ashworth, *The Economic History of England 1870-1939* (Methuen, 1972)

Lord Askwith, *Industrial Disputes* (John Murray, 1920)

Lord Beaverbrook, *Men and Power 1917-18* (Hutchinson, 1956)

Sir Thomas Beecham, *A Mingled Chime* (Hutchinson, 1974)

Arnold Bennett, *Journals*, Vol. 2, 1911-21 (Cassell, 1932)

Robert Blake, *The Unknown Prime Minister* (Eyre & Spottiswoode, 1955)

Edmund Blunden, *Undertones of War* (Collins, 1965)

Asa Briggs, *Social Thought and Social Action, A Study of Seebohm Rowntree* (Longman, 1961)

Asa Briggs (Ed.), *They Saw It Happen, 1897-1940* (Basil Blackwell, 1960)

Vera Brittain, *Testament of Youth* (Gollancz, 1933)

Frank P. Chambers, *The War behind the War* (Faber, 1939)

L.E.O. Charlton, *War Over England* (Longman, 1938)

G.K. Chesterton, *Autobiography* (Hutchinson, 1936)

Randolph Churchill, *Lord Derby* (Heinemann, 1959)

Winston Churchill, *The World Crisis* (Butterworth, 1923)

J.R. Clynes, *Memoirs* (Hutchinson, 1937)

G.D.H. Cole & R.W. Postgate, *The Common People 1746-1946* (Methuen, 1965)

Deward David (Ed.), *Inside Asquith's Cabinet (from the diaries of Charles Hobhouse)* (John Murray, 1977)

N.B. Dearle, *An Economic Chronicle of the Great War* (Oxford University Press, 1929)

D.F. Fleming, *The Origins and Legacies of World War I* (Allen & Unwin, 1969)

Sir Philip Gibbs, *Realities of War* (Heinemann, 1920)

Martin Gilbert, *Winston S. Churchill* (Vols. 3 & 4) (Heinemann, 1971 and 1975)

Robert Graves, *Goodbye to All That* (Jonathan Cape, 1929)

Pauline Gregg, *A Social and Economic History of Britain, 1760-1950* (George G. Harrap)

Lord Grey of Falloden, *Twenty-five Years* (Hodder & Stoughton, 1925)

C. Haste, *Keep the Home Fires Burning* (Allen Lane, 1977)

S.J. Hurwitz, *State Intervention in Great Britain, 1914-19* (Cassell, 1968)

Roy Jenkins, *Asquith* (Collins, 1964)

Denis Judd, *The Life and Times of George V* (Weidenfeld and Nicolson, 1973)

D.H. Lawrence, *Kangaroo* (1923) (Penguin, 1950)

David Lloyd George, *War Memoirs* (Odhams Press, 1936)

Michael MacDonagh, *In London during the Great War* (Eyre & Spottiswoode, 1935)

Stephen McKenna, *While I Remember* (Butterworth, 1921)

Philip Magnus, *Kitchener* (John Murray, 1958)

Harold Macmillan, *Winds of Change* (Macmillan, 1966)

Arthur Marwick, *The Deluge* (The Bodley Head, 1965)

C.F.G. Masterman, *England after the War* (Hodder & Stoughton, 1922)

W.N. Medlicott, *Contemporary England 1914-64* (Longman, 1967)

David Mitchell, *Women on the Warpath* (Jonathan Cape, 1966)

C.E. Montagu, *Disenchantment* (Chatto and Windus, 1922)

Oswald Mosley, *My Life* (Nelson, 1968)

C.L. Mowat, *Great Britain since 1914* (Cambridge University Press, 1976)

Harold Nicolson, *King George V* (Constable, 1952)

V. Ogilvie, *Our Times 1912-1952* (Batsford, 1953)

Baroness Orczy, *Links in the Chain of Life* (Hutchinson, 1947)

Frank Owen, *Tempestuous Journey* (Hutchinson, 1954)

Sylvia Pankhurst, *The Home Front* (Hutchinson, 1932)

I.M. Parsons (Ed.), *Men Who March Away* (Chatto & Windus, 1965)

Mrs. C.S. Peel, *How We Lived Then* (John Lane, The Bodley Head, 1929)

Henry Pelling, *Winston Churchill* (Macmillan, 1974)

Sir Charles Petrie, *A Historian Looks at his World* (Sidgwick and Jackson, 1972)

C.E. Playne, *Society at War* (Allen & Unwin, 1931)

Sir Frederick Ponsonby, *Recollections of Three Reigns* (Eyre & Spottiswoode, 1951)

Reginald Pound and Geoffrey Harmsworth, *Northcliffe* (Cassell, 1959)

J.B. Priestley, *English Journey* (Heinemann, 1934)

Mr Punch's History of the Great War (Cassell, 1919)

C.B. Purdom (Ed.), *Everyman at War* (Dent, 1930)

John Rae, *Conscience and Politics* (Oxford University Press, 1970)

Lt-Col. C. Repington, *The First World War* (Constable, 1920)

Robert Rhodes James, *The British Revolution*, Vol. 2, 1914-39 (Hamish Hamilton, 1977)

Siegfried Sassoon, *Memoirs of an Infantry Officer* (Faber, 1965)

G.B. Shaw, *Heartbreak House* (Constable, 1919)

R.C. Sheriff, *Journey's End* (Gollancz, 1929)

Sir Osbert Sitwell, *Great Morning* (Macmillan, 1948) *Laughter in the Next Room* (Macmillan, 1949)

D.C. Somervell, *Modern Britain 1870-1939* (Methuen, 1941)

Frances Stevenson, *Lloyd George, A Diary* (Hutchinson, 1971)

G.S. Street, *At Home in the War* (Heinemann, 1918)

Helena Swanwick, *I have been young* (Gollancz, 1935)

Julian Symons, *Horatio Bottomley* (Cresset Press, 1955)

A.J.P. Taylor, *English History 1914-45* (Oxford University Press, 1965)

Daivd Thomson, *England in the Twentieth Century* (Penguin, 1965)

The Times History of the War, 1914-18 (22 vols)

G.M. Trevelyan, *Grey of Falloden* (Longmans, Green, 1937)

Barbara Tuchman, *August 1914* (Constable, 1962)

E.S. Turner, *Dear Old Blighty* (Michael Joseph, 1980)

H.G. Wells, *Mr Britling Sees it Through* (Cassell, 1916)

John Williams, *The Home Fronts* (Constable, 1972)

Leonard Woolf, *Beginning Again, 1911-18* (The Hogarth Press, 1964)

INDEX